HOME MADE
simple

HOME MADE
simple

Stylish, practical makes
for living and giving

JOANNA GOSLING

Photography by Rachel Whiting

Kyle Books

for Mum and Granny, my domestic goddesses

First published in Great Britain in 2013 by
Kyle Books
67–69 Whitfield Street
London, W1T 4HF
general.enquiries@kylebooks.com
www.kylebooks.com

ISBN: 978-0-85783-100-2

Text © 2013 Joanna Gosling
Photographs © 2013 Rachel Whiting
Design © 2013 Kyle Books

Designer: Jenny Semple
Photographer: Rachel Whiting
Photographer's assistants: Rita Platts and Corin Ashleigh Brown
Props stylist: Victoria Fitchett
Editor: Catharine Robertson
Copy editor: Liz Lemal
Proofreader: Salima Hirani
Index: Helen Snaith
Production: Lisa Pinnell

A Cataloguing In Publication record for this title is available from the British Library.

Printed and bound in China by C&C Offset Printing Company Ltd.

CONTENTS

I love old wine boxes – so easily transformed into something stylish and useful.

Making is a time
to breathe.
To think. Or not.
Just to be.

INTRODUCTION

This is a book about homemade made easy.
Simple makes – no special skills required.

This book is about making your own because you can make nicer than you can buy, and because the process of doing so is pleasurable. And it is about simplifying your life, stripping away the constant bombardment of material things we are tempted to believe we need. When you spend a little bit of time and effort making something, it helps you to evaluate what is important – need versus want.

I have been making things for as long as I can remember. My projects have always had the same starting point – an idea of something specific I'd like, then a logical way around making it simply, to achieve the effect (albeit not always perfectly).

I remember wanting a pair of baggy floral trousers when I was about twelve. Without a pattern or any real know-how, I simply cut out the fabric, using an existing pair of trousers as a basic guide for size, then painstakingly sewed them by hand. Inside they were very rough and ready, but on the outside I'd got the style I wanted. So the lack of a professional finish didn't matter and I wore them to death.

Since then I've taught myself how to use a sewing machine, so sewing projects are a lot quicker, but still the same principle applies. Whatever I want to make, I work out the quickest, simplest way to do it. I have loads of creative ideas, but – like most of us – not enough time to sit and spend hours crafting something perfectly, so my mantra is always, 'Minimum effort, maximum return'.

Not many days go by when I don't make something – for the home, for me or for someone else. Friends and family always ask how I do it – both in the 'how to' sense and how I find the time to do it. My answer is always that I do things the easy way – nothing takes long to do. I think a desire to simplify everything comes from my journalistic background – or maybe that's why I went into journalism. That job's about making the complicated accessible, which is exactly what I do at home.

So this book is all about making things simply, so that you derive pleasure from the process as well as the end result and don't stress about not being able to do it 'properly'. I like the fact that homemade isn't always perfect. It gives character.

One of the simplest ways of making is to transform something that's already been made and used for something else. An abandoned wooden pallet, an old wine box, jam jars, pegs, shells, pine cones... with some imagination and a little bit of effort, these can be turned into something fabulous. And for free – or at least for a fraction of the cost of buying something similar, but invariably not as nice. For instance, my pallet tables, which were made because the only coffee tables I ever saw for sale that I liked were fiendishly expensive. These super-simple tables cost little to make, but I love them – not just because they're stylish and look great, but also because every time I see them I have the added 'I made that' satisfaction.

The Japanese word for doing this is *mottainai*, which roughly translates as 'it's a shame for something to go to waste without its full potential having been made use of'. How brilliant is that? One word that encapsulates so much more than the term 'upcycling'. Once you start to contemplate things in this way, it is amazing how many items can be used for something other than that which they were designed for – and it is so satisfying.

Chapter 1 of this book, the home section, includes a lot of *mottainai* DIY makes. These are practical, useful makes for around the house. But nothing involves anything more complicated than drilling holes. Everything can be done very easily using a basic drill and screwdrivers, but if you have a good electric drill/screwdriver, even better. The same is true for a sewing machine for stitching projects – a good one of these is life-changing in the amount of time and effort it will save.

Chapter 2, the giving section, is more crafty in the traditional sense and includes knitting, stitching, candle making and cooking. The same 'keep it simple' ethic applies though. Where the building blocks of the *mottainai* projects are reused items, the building blocks of the knitted projects, for instance, are basic squares or rectangles – quick and easy to whip up, no complicated patterns to follow, but put together to be greater than the sum of their parts. I like to give practical presents, whether it's something that will make life easier, or a little brighter – like candles – because I know they will be put to use, so again, everything in this section is practical but pretty.

Finally chapter 3, the celebration section, includes a mix of *mottainai* and making from scratch. It covers the elements of celebration – the decorations and some of the foods that are an integral part of holiday times. The rituals and traditions of all cultures and religions are such a great source of inspiration. It's a bit like brilliant household tips. What you know and do might seem obvious to you – part of the routine – but if you pass it on to someone else who's never come across it before, it can be life-changing. That's what I love about learning from other cultures. The *furoshiki* knotted bags, for instance. Second nature in Japan, but barely known elsewhere. They are genius. Other elements of this section are not unique to different cultures, but I love that, too. As the saying goes, there is so much more that unites us than divides us. Everything can be used by anyone, any time, to bring a simple decorative – or delicious – element to celebrations, or even every day.

Don't knock yourself out trying to shoehorn sourcing everything and putting it together in one day if it's going to make your head explode. One of the key messages of my first book, *Simply Wonderwoman*, was 'everything in small steps – one thing each day'. This applies as much to making lovely things as to the boring stuff that has to be done, but that can fill your entire headspace and time if you're not careful. So, I break down the making process to keep it simple and stress-free. To make life easiest on the sourcing front, I tend to buy most bits and pieces online. I'll order things in a brief quiet moment, ready to have to hand for when I've a little bit more time to piece them together. When I'm out and about, I buy pretty things as I see them, such as unusual ingredients, fabric, ribbon, thread, elastic. Similarly, for a bigger project, such as the wine crate desk, I build it up in increments. Get the MDF cut at a timber yard one day. On another, get hold of the wine crates. I'll pick up the castors and wood glue when I'm passing a large DIY store. Gather things slowly so that when you sit down to actually make something, there's no stress about having to rush out and get the ingredients. You can just enjoy the process of making. Making is about pleasure – not pressure. Making is a time to breathe. To think. Or not. Just to be.

'Have nothing in your home which you do not know to be useful or consider to be beautiful'

WILLIAM MORRIS

USEFUL EQUIPMENT

Listed below are some of my favourite tools. Some are included because I use them all the time, others because they make life easier.

SEWING MACHINE – If you don't own a sewing machine, and have never used one before, please don't be daunted by the prospect.

Forget the ultra-fancy machines that do so many stitches and tricks it's bamboozling. All you need is a simple machine that does the basics – straight stitch in varying lengths and reverse stitch. I don't think I have ever used my machine for anything other than these. I have tried to machine stitch buttonholes, but found it too laborious to be worth bothering with, so returned to my default 'cheat's' sewing mode of never sewing in buttons – unless I use a loop to secure them.

Using a machine to do straight stitch back and forth needs no lessons, just a quick scan of the manual and some common sense. You'll be up and running in no time.

If you are planning to buy a machine, I recommend you go for one that has a transparent top-loading bobbin system. It's a cinch to drop in the bobbin and you can see through the transparent window when it's running out of thread. Absolutely brilliant. I hated my old machine's traditional front loading system, where you insert the bobbin and then can't see it, so you're constantly wondering whether you're about to run out of thread.

If you're going to be sewing at the kitchen table, or somewhere you'll need to pack up when you're done, go for a lightweight machine, so that it's not such a palaver to have to pick up and put away. If you have a quiet space where it can live and be used, there's no need to worry about that.

FABRIC can be ridiculously expensive to buy, but there are plenty of ways of getting gorgeous fabric at low prices. Here are some of my favourite sources:

- Warehouse sales
- Jumble sales/thrift shops – old curtains and clothes can be a great source of cheap, funky, quality fabric
- Your own old clothes
- Independent fabric shops and market stalls
- Offcuts – always ask to see the remnants box in any fabric shop, which often can be a real treasure trove!
- If there is a particular fabric you feel you can't live without, search online auction sites for offcuts. A little persistence often pays off.

WINE BOXES – I love to use old wooden wine boxes. They come practically for free and, with a teensy bit of effort, they can be transformed into something so stylish and useful. Getting hold of them depends on a little bit of luck. Try wine warehouses, wine stores and even supermarkets for discarded boxes. When I first started getting them from my local wine warehouse, they would give them to me for free and there was normally a fairly plentiful supply. Now I sometimes have to put my name down for them and there's a fixed (albeit nominal) fee per box. Christmas time is always a good season to obtain wine boxes as people are splashing out on the expensive wine that is supplied in them.

If you can't find a local source of unwanted boxes, you can buy them direct from suppliers. They'll be more expensive, but this is still way cheaper than buying similar-sized wooden boxes from anywhere else. Do an online search on 'cheap 12-bottle wooden wine box' and shop around.

ELECTRIC POWER DRILL/SCREWDRIVER – If you are going to do a lot of DIY and making, a really good combined power drill and screwdriver is definitely worth buying (or requesting as a present). Get a decent set of drill bits and driver heads to go with it.

Armed with a sewing machine and a power drill, you can make almost anything.

HOME MADE *home*

As a practical creature to the core, everything I make is useful. Equally, I like the basic necessities around the house to be nice to look at. Somehow, it makes using them more pleasing.

For me, a homemade home isn't about crafty nick-nacks that gather dust, but practical items that I have made myself. For example, a fresh coat of paint is the most straightforward and obvious way of changing a room. A painted floor. A simple panel of fabric at a window, or to cover messy storage. A peg stuck to my front door to hold things I mustn't forget. Candles galore. And a myriad of old objects re-styled and re-used. Little things that make a big difference.

As ever, it's about doing things the easy way, for minimum effort, maximum return...

PINLIGHT CANVAS

I got inspiration for this project as I walked through a dank underpass decorated with lights peeping through holes in a long strip of metal. It looked so cool, making a normally gloomy, unloved place memorable. So this is my very simple version, which can be made with no electrical or metal-working skills. As with the underpass, you can use it to breathe life into a dark corner, or let it be a centre-stage statement.

I've kept my design ultra simple – a heart. It's easy to do, and I heart hearts. A star would be fab too – and just as easy. Or try any shape you like.

you will need

Canvas – my canvas measures 70cm x 60cm, but as with all the makes in this book, there are no rules here – scale up or down to fit the wall space

Drill with 2mm drill bit, or a bradawl

Battery-operated LED pin lights with 30–50 bulbs, depending on canvas size and personal taste

Medium-duty general purpose wire for hanging

Wire cutters

Ruler

Staple gun or 2 round hooks

Method

1 Draw a light pencil outline on the back of the canvas. Don't worry if you need to redraw the lines – you won't see it on the front.

2 When you're happy with your shape, you need to mark where the bulbs will go. They should be fairly evenly spaced, so halve your number of lights and mark two points opposite each other on the shape that would effectively cut a line halfway through it. Next, mark dots for each bulb in between. So, if you have 30 bulbs, you would need to mark 14 points in between each of the first two marks. Just do it by eye – there's no need to be exact. Before you go on, count up your dots just to be sure you've got the right number.

3 Now you need to make little holes where each dot is. You could use either a 2mm drill bit, or a bradawl (a thin, pointed metal tool) to make these. The holes should be smaller than the bulbs, so that you need to force them through, which will hold them in place. Push each bulb in as you go.

4 Fix a wire onto the back of the canvas to hang it on the wall. The quickest and easiest way to do this is with a staple gun. Doing it this way also has the added bonus of fixing the wire flush with the frame, so it will sit flat against the wall. Using wire cutters, cut a length of wire as wide as the frame, plus 15cm. This will leave long ends at either side that can be twisted around the wire to make sure it stays in place. Staple the wire onto each side of the frame at the height you want, using several staples to make sure it is fixed firmly. Then twist the long ends of the wire back around the stretched part so that it holds tight. If you don't have a staple gun, screw round hooks into the top inside edges of the frame to fix the wire to. Again, this will allow the frame to sit flush against the wall.

5 Hang your canvas and sit the battery pack inside the frame, on the bottom ledge. When you want to turn the lights on and off, pull the frame away from the wall slightly so that you can reach the switch. Obviously, the bulbs are not glued in place, so if any of them pull through the holes when you move the frame, just pop them back through. But they should stay put if you are gentle.

★ HOME ★

⋆ ⋆ ⋆

WINE CRATE DESK

I love this desk. It is such a practical design, with its internal storage, big surface area and castors that make it easy to move around. It makes a perfect work space for anything from writing to crafting. The streamlined shelving created by the crates will store books or anything else you want to hand, but they will be tucked away neatly.

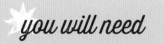
you will need

Strong wood glue

4 x 12-bottle wine crates

2 sheets of 30mm MDF measuring 505mm x 175mm and 1 sheet of MDF measuring 505mm x 1460mm (or however wide you want it to fit your space)

8 x 50mm castors

32 x 1cm screws for the castors

Drill with 2mm and 4mm drill bit

12 x 6cm screws

Paint – preferably eggshell for the top surface for its durability

Roller and small paintbrush

I just had to design a wine crate desk after a colleague told me how, when he was a boy, his dad had made one for him. It was a story that stuck. We do so many things for our kids – as our parents did for us – but so much of it is lost in the past and I always wonder what it is that makes one particular thing or moment lodge in the memory while others drift away. So the wine crate desk – a borrowed childhood memory – burned itself into my mind. I'd imagined the RDD (Robert's dad's desk) to be made entirely of wine crates, but I couldn't make that work. So my version is a combination of wine crates and cheap MDF. It means it's not entirely free to construct, but it is still way cheaper than buying anything even remotely as stylish.

Method

1 Make the two end supports for the desk. Glue the long sides of two wine crates together to make one support, and repeat with the other two for the second support. Make sure the glue gets a good fix by piling some heavy books inside the top crate to press it downwards onto the lower one.

2 Place the large sheet of MDF on the floor. Position one small piece of MDF at either end of the large piece and align the edges. Glue the small pieces in place using plenty of glue. Now position the end supports on top of each of these small sheets of MDF, ensuring the interiors of the crates are facing inwards. Glue these in place. This is the basic construction of the desk upside down.

3 Position four castors on the corners of the base of each end support and screw them on. Using the 2mm drill bit, drill small holes into the wood through the holes in the castor plates for the screws to go into.

4 Now switch to the 4mm drill bit and drill six holes through the top wine crates into the MDF (one at each corner and two in the middle for strength). This is for the 6cm screws, to fix the base to the desk top. Position the screw against the drill bit when you fix the bit into the drill. Make the length of the drill bit slightly shorter than the screw, so that you don't drill too deeply and go right through the desk top. Screw together.

5 Once the glue fixing the wine crates together is dry, flip the desk over. It is heavy, so get someone to help you if possible.

6 Finally, paint the desk using a roller. I love this desk. Thanks, Robert's dad.

WINE CRATE DESK TIDY

This crate provides a simple way of keeping your desk or work space clutter-free and combines two of my favourite and most versatile upcycling basics – a wooden wine crate and a large peg. Papers and other loose bits can go in the box and anything you want immediately to hand, such as reminder notes, stamps, letters to post or pictures, can be fixed onto the outside of the box using the peg.

you will need

6-bottle wine crate – the sort that holds 2 layers of 3 bottles rather than all 6 flat

Pliers

Paint – emulsion or eggshell, depending whether you want it matt or with a sheen

Mini roller and small paintbrush

Large peg

Scrap of fabric or wallpaper to cover the peg (optional)

Double-sided tape (optional)

Strong wood glue

Method

1 Remove any rogue staples that have been left behind from where the lid was fixed onto the box originally using a pair of pliers. A little twist and a yank should whip them out with no sweat. It's a good idea to vacuum the insides of the box quickly just to get rid of any dust or loose wood. For the quickest, easiest version, simply paint the box inside and out. You don't need much paint, so just use whatever leftovers you've got. I always paint with a mini roller as it's the quickest way and gives a nice smooth finish. Just use a brush to cover the parts the roller won't reach.

2 Now either paint your peg or fix fabric or wallpaper onto the front and back using double-sided tape. Then put some extra-strong glue on the bottom third of the back of the peg, covering the area just below where the groove is for the spring. Fix the peg to the front of your box and leave to dry.

 Having one of these on my desk means there's somewhere to stash paperwork until I've got time to deal with it.

FABRIC-COVERED DESK TIDY

An especially gorgeous version of the box shown on page 19 is one that is covered with fabric. This makes a really lovely gift, especially if you use a pretty fabric such as a Liberty print. It does take longer to make than the simple version, but it isn't difficult.

you will need

The same materials used to make the wine crate desk tidy (see page 18) plus about ½ m fabric.

Fabric scissors and a craft knife

Fabric-covered mouse mat

While you're on a roll with the double-sided tape and scraps of fabric, why not make a quick mouse mat, just to really raise the style stakes on your desk?! This is something I've always done, because I've never found a mouse mat to buy that I would actually want on my desk. I've tried not using them, but then the scrapey noise is annoying. I guess they were invented for a reason, even if they've spawned an industry of tasteless desk tat. Anyway, either use your current one, or buy a real cheapy. Cover it with strips of double-sided tape. Fix a piece of fabric on top. Trim to size. Isn't that so much better?

Method

1 First, cut a rectangle of fabric to fit the inner base of the box. To cut fabric to size, place the box on the fabric and draw around the edges. The cut shape will be slightly larger than the inside measurement, but you can very easily trim away the excess with a craft knife once the fabric is fixed in place.

2 Do the same for the four inner sides of the box, although add an extra 1.5cm to the height for each side. This is to cover the top edge of the box.

3 Stick the fabric in place with double-sided tape (glue would seep through the material and spoil it). Position strips of tape around the four sides of the outer base, then fix the fabric to the base. Press down firmly and trim away the excess with a very sharp craft knife.

4 When you are fixing the rest of the fabric to the inside of the box, put extra tape along the top lip of the box. Fix the fabric on the inside and then pull it firmly across the top edge of the box so that it fans around each corner slightly, otherwise you'll end up with little uncovered squares on each of the top four corners. Trim away the excess.

5 Finally, fix tape all the way round the outside top and bottom of the box, plus strips down each vertical edge. Cut a long rectangle of fabric that will be big enough to go the whole way round the outside of the box. Don't worry about making it exact; you can easily trim it down with sharp scissors once it's on. Better too big than too small, because you can't fix that. Don't worry about finishing the edges of the fabric – too much faff! These projects are all about doing things quickly and easily. Plus, I love the imperfection of raw, frayed edges.

If you are giving this as a gift, you could peg a note to the front and put some little treats inside the box.

TIP When you're fixing the fabric onto the tape, just pull a little of the backing off the tape as you go, to make it easier to fix the fabric on straight. Don't worry if you mess up. You can pull away the fabric and reposition it.

PALLET COFFEE TABLE

Whenever I see an abandoned pallet in the street, it makes me start to dream of what I could turn it into. I'm pretty sure you could almost build a whole house with them and then create all the furniture you need to fill it up. Keeping it simple, I offer up instead a couple of basic pieces, which are well worth making because they are practically free to create and do look really great. The most obvious thing of all is a simple coffee table.

If you've got pallet options, such as a local builder's yard, or someone nearby having building work done (meaning a ready supply of pallets), be picky and opt for the sort that has two rows of slats, sandwiched together. This type is perfect for a low coffee table, because it allows you to slide magazines and books on the bottom 'shelf' for a 'deluxe' version. Otherwise, any pallet will do.

you will need

Pallet

Sandpaper, medium grade

Paint – personally, I like a matt emulsion, as anything with a bit of sheen draws even more attention to imperfections and the roughness of the wood

Roller and small paintbrush

4 x large castors

Pen or pencil

Drill and 2mm drill bit

16 x 1cm screws

Method

1 If the pallet is damp and/or dirty – which it probably will be – bring it into the house and stand it on its side somewhere warmish for a couple of days so it can dry out completely.

2 Once the dirt has dried, most of it should come off pretty easily with a quick blast of the vacuum cleaner. If it's engrained, don't worry about it – you'll be able to paint over it – it's just the loose bits that the paint won't stick to. Now sand over the pallet a little, just to get rid of giant splinters. You are not trying to sand it down to a smooth finish, which would take forever. This IS going to look pretty rustic, as pallets are made of rough wood.

3 Now paint the pallet. It's easiest to roller on the paint and use a small brush for the little fiddly bits the roller won't reach. Start by laying the pallet flat on top of some sort of protective floor covering and raise it off the ground by sticking four evenly sized items (building blocks, books, bricks, whatever you've got) under each corner. Once the top is done, stand it up on its side to make it easier to reach the bottom slats.

4 When the paint is dry, screw a large castor onto each of the bottom corners of the pallet. The 1cm screws won't go all the way through the slats. To make light work of fixing the screws, mark through the four holes on the castor plate and then drill small holes over your markings. Drill gently so that the drill bit doesn't go right through the wood. After 20 years of DIY I've finally invested in a good cordless drill/driver with lithium batteries and a full set of bits and, I must say, it is heavenly. Job done in a flash. I just say this to recommend it as a gadget really worth having. But don't worry if you don't have one. It's perfectly easy to do this job with a basic drill and normal screwdriver – it's what I've always done in the past. It will just take a bit longer and might make your wrist ache a little. But, hey – you can sit back with a nice cup of tea and a mag and put your feet up on your groovy new table once you're done. Pretty satisfying.

POSH PALLET TABLE

I think of this as the 'fur coat, no knickers' table. In other words, it looks quite classy on the outside, but you've spent nothing on what's underneath, unseen.

you will need

Tape measure

Large pallet – if you want a higher, chunkier table, you could sandwich two pallets together using wood glue

Fabric – about 2m

2m² sheet of 1cm-thick foam (see resources, page 157)

Staple gun

4 x large castors

Drill and 2.5mm drill bit

16 x 2.5cm screws

It doesn't matter how tatty your pallet is as it will be covered, but make sure it is dry and that any loose dirt has been vacuumed off before you get to work. If you don't already have a staple gun, you can buy one very cheaply from any hardware store. They are perfectly good and will do the job. The only downside with a cheapie gun is that the staples don't always go in firmly enough, so it sometimes requires a bit of firing, pulling out and firing again. I used that sort for years before I finally bought a decent one (which is better to use, but is more expensive) from an upholstery shop, so do weigh up what you're prepared to spend. I would say, once you're armed with one, there'll probably be no stopping you. I use a staple gun loads for quick repairs and cheeky upholstery jobs, going with my usual 'minimum effort, maximum return' mantra. More on that later (see page 30)...

Scatter some coffee table books and magazines on your table. Some flowers. Maybe a pretty tray and a candle. Boutique hotel style on a shoestring.

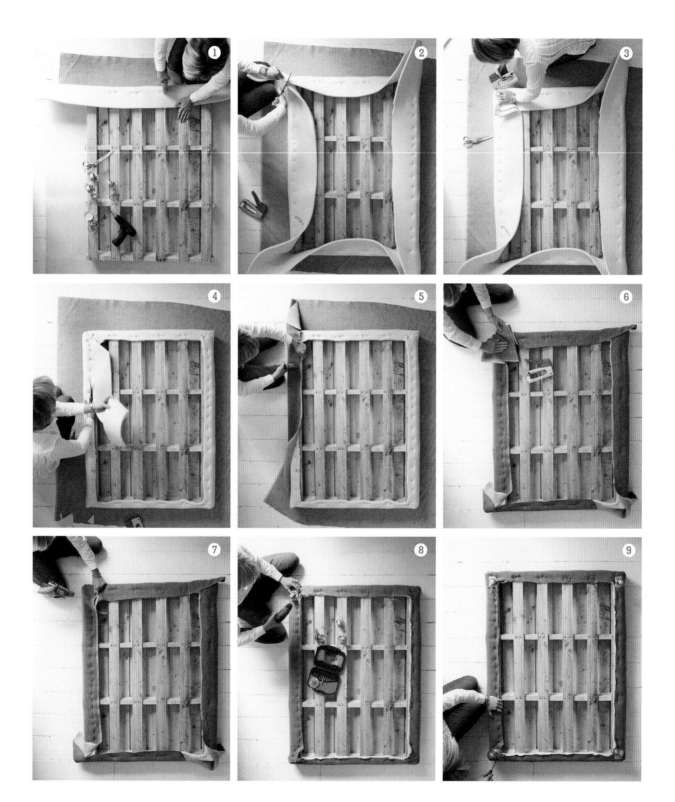

To check the dimensions of the fabric, measure up one side of the pallet(s), along the top edge, and down the opposite side, then add 20cm to allow extra fabric for the foam (which will go underneath the fabric), and for stapling the fabric to the underside of the pallet. Do the same measurements the other way across the pallet. You should end up with a measurement approximately 165cm x 125cm. So 2m of fabric should be plenty and might give you enough left over to make a matching cushion cover or two.

Method

1 Place the fabric on the floor with the right side facing down. Lay the foam sheet on top of the fabric and, finally, put the upturned pallet(s), centred, on top. Pull up one edge of the foam to prepare to staple it to the underside of the pallet. Now the fun part. Fire off a row of staples 2cm apart and about 4cm in from the edge. Do the same with opposite edge of the foam. Lift the pallet up slightly and pull the foam before you staple, to be sure it is lying flat and snug across the wood, but not too tight so that you see the ridges of the planks beneath.Staple the foam in place as before. Repeat with the remaining two edges of the foam.

2 You will have folded flaps of foam on each corner. Carefully cut these away so that the foam lies flat with no overlap, but no gaps, either.

3 Staple the cut corners to the underside of the pallet.

4 Cut away the excess foam on the underside of the pallet, cutting a centimetre or two away from the staples.

5 You use a very similar stapling trick with the fabric. Pull up one edge of the fabric and staple this to the underside of the pallet over the foam, ensuring you pull the fabric taut before stapling down the opposite edge. The only thing is, don't staple along the full length of each side – leave a gap of about 15cm at each corner. This is to allow you to fold the fabric on the corner to make a nice neat, professional-looking finish.

6 Once you've stapled down each edge and the fabric is taut, finish the corners with an inverse pleat. Pull the corner point of the fabric in towards the centre, then fold the sides neatly up against the corner of the pallet, to make a smart pleat.

7 Staple the pleated corner to the pallet.

8 Finally, screw on the castors. You will need to drill through the fabric and foam to get them on, but it's not difficult. Hold a castor in place on one corner of the underside of the pallet and drill through one hole with a 2.5mm drill bit.

9 Fix a screw through the hole to keep the castor in place. Repeat with the three other holes, then with each castor.

FABRIC CABLE LIGHTS

If you can wire a plug you can make one of these brilliant lights very easily. If you can't wire a plug, don't worry, it is so easy to learn and to get up and running with very basic electrical jobs.

Apart from the fact that they look great, the thing I love about these lights is that they are so versatile and useful. Make the cable as long as you like and, with a couple of hooks on the ceiling, you can fix them to light up anywhere in a room. And you can position them high or low, as you want. Plus, the bits and pieces required can be bought very cheaply, so it is definitely a make that gives you maximum bang for your buck.

Method

1 First, open up the lamp holder by unscrewing the top and bottom to separate. Feed the top of the lamp holder onto the cable. Strip the wires (take care not to expose too much wire). Wire the cable to the bottom of the lamp holder. With a three-core cable, which includes live, neutral and earth wires, there will be a point in the side of the fitting to connect the earth wire to. The live and neutral wires can safely be connected to either of the other points. Screw the two parts of the lamp holder together.

2 Now strip the wires at the other end of the cable and connect to the plug. Make sure you connect the wires to the correct points. Even though I've wired loads of plugs, I always double check the correct wiring by doing an internet image search on 'how to wire a plug'. It will bring up clear diagrams, so you can be absolutely certain of getting it right.

Once the wiring's done, just plug and play.

If you're nervous about wiring, why not get a friend or relative to whip this up for you? For anyone confident about wiring a plug, it's super quick and easy to do.

you will need

For countries that use the 3-pin plug:

Switched metal lamp holder

Fabric-covered 3-core cable – measure the length you will need

Cable stripper and small screwdriver

3-pin plug

Bulb – make sure it is compatible with the lamp holder (ie. screw or bayonet). Do an online image search for '(either bayonet or screw) filament light bulb', to see a gorgeous range of options

Screw hooks to suspend the light from the ceiling

For countries that use the 2-pin plug:

Switched metal lamp holder

Fabric-covered 2-core cable – measure the length you will need

Cable stripper and small screwdriver

2-pin plug

Bulb – make sure it is compatible with the lamp holder (ie. screw or bayonet). (See above)

Screw hooks to suspend the light from the ceiling

★★★ BASIC UPHOLSTERY

Armed with a basic staple gun, the possibilities for quick, easy upholstery are endless. So to get you thinking, here are a couple of examples of things I've done...

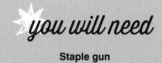

you will need

Staple gun

Fabric

Fabric scissors

A scruffy old sofa (See picture on page 28)

Ridiculously, I admit, I bought a sofa with loose white covers... when we have three children?! I fell for a 'tip' I read somewhere years ago that white covers are actually practical because you can boil wash them to get them looking like new. Well, here's another tip: if you've got small kids, don't ever believe anyone who tells you white covers are practical. They'll be off the sofa cushions more than they're on and will definitely shrink when boil washed. So, having long ago ditched the nightmarish white covers that had been washed and shrunk so many times that putting them on was like dressing the Incredible Hulk, I finally had a eureka moment – and this idea will work for any unloved sofa... I bought cheap hessian and did a quick staple job. Fabulous.

It goes without saying that all sofas are different – or at least the chances that you have exactly the same as me are slim. In other words, there's no point in me telling you exactly how to do this – like a recipe – because, like any practical cook, you're going to have to adapt it to your own needs. I won't lie to you. This can be slightly tricky (depending on the shape of your sofa – I did one that was dead simple, another much less so), but if you have an ugly old settee you're sick of the sight of, I reckon it's worth spending a couple of hours with a staple gun and some fabric to transform it. So here are some guidelines on how to do it.

For this sofa, which measures 70cm x 85cm x 210cm, I bought 10m of fabric. CHEAP fabric. This is a rough and ready job, so keep the background cheap and cheerful and jazz it up with cushions and throws. Hessian is great because it is ULTRA cheap, but looks really stylish as a fitted cover. Plus it avoids the twitchiness associated with fitted covers because if it gets stained, it's so cheap, it's no sweat to staple a bit more on top. Or pull off a bit and redo.

If your sofa has arms like mine, break it down into four separate upholstery jobs. Start with each arm. Then do the back and then the front. Of course, you can ignore bits that won't be seen if that's easier. If the sofa doesn't have arms, break it into two sections – the back and then the base.

Method

1 First, drape the fabric over the area you are covering to make sure it properly covers it. Don't make any cuts at all until the fabric is draped in place and you've anchored it with the first staples. If the sofa has curved arms like mine, it is best to start stapling the fabric tight into the underside of the curve in the arm. Then pull it taut and staple it on the underside of the sofa. Before stapling feel where the wooden frame is so that you staple into that, or the staples won't hold.

2 Now pull the fabric flat over the top of the arm and staple it on the inside of the frame. Now you can make your first cuts. Don't forget, it's always best to cut too little at first than too much, so go easy. Basically, you want enough fabric to allow for it to cover the entire side section, with the edge of the fabric folded underneath (like an unstitched hem) to make it neat. Play around with the fabric where it bunches up, either folding it like a parcel or gathering it, whichever works best. Repeat with the opposite end of the sofa. Those are the hardest parts. The back and front should be pretty straightforward. If you've got a sofa without arms, it will be a cinch.

3 Don't worry about sewing new covers for the seat cushions. Just wrap a piece of fabric around them.

Finish off with a throw or two and a pile of cushions (see page 28). I made these super quickly using old grain and potato sacks. Simply machine stitch around three sides, turn the right way out and insert the cushion. Then fold in the rough edges on the open side and machine stitch as close to the edge as you can – there's no need for zips. They can be thrown into the washing machine, cushion and all.

A chair base

The quickest and easiest make-do upholstery job of them all – a drop-in seat from a chair. Simply lift it out. Pull a piece of fabric taut over the seat. Staple around the underside of the seat, making sure the fabric is pulled taut. Done.

Easy peasy.

> I can't exhaust all the options here. I simply urge you to think about the possibilities when eyeing up a piece of ugly upholstery while tooled up with a staple gun and a scrap of fabric.

A stool...

I transformed an ugly stool by simply covering the seat in a small linen offcut and stapling it on the underside to hold it firm. Normally, I go for loose covers on seats and sofas for practicality, so they can go in the washing machine – I reckon kids plus fixed upholstery equals twitchiness that life is too short for. However, when something's this simple to do, who cares if someone spills juice all over it or the cat uses it as a scratch pad? Just whip it off and redo. If you want to add extra padding to the seat, staple an offcut of upholstery foam (or even layer up several pieces for more cushioning) over the seat first.

★★★ WALL-HUNG BOOKCASES

Old wine crates make perfect wall-hung bookcases and shelving units. They look great dotted around or buttressed right up against each other in a stack or a row.

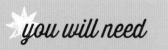 you will need

Wine crates

Paint – eggshell or emulsion

Roller and small paintbrush

Drill and 3.5mm and 7mm or 7.5mm drill bits

Spirit level

4 x size 8 all-purpose or universal rawl plugs per box

4 x 4cm long screws per box

Floating bedside box

Functional, stylish and, I think, miles hipper than most bedside tables/cabinets you can buy.

you will need

**6- or 12-bottle wine box
Paint**

Just follow the wall-hung bookcases 'how to' (see right), but fix them in line with the side of the bed. Now just add books and a mug of tea, curl up in bed and enjoy.

Method

1 Transforming these just requires a very quick and easy paint job. Either eggshell or matt paints are fine – whichever you have to hand and like best. Two coats should do. As usual, for speed and the best finish, use a roller and in-fill with a brush.

2 Drill four holes in the back of your bookcase – one in each of the corners. Position each hole so that it is 10cm from the edges. Use a 3.5mm drill bit. The holes must be big enough to allow the body of the screw to go through, but not the head.

3 Place a spirit level on the box and hold it up to the wall in the position which you intend to hang your bookcase. When it is level, poke a sharp pencil through the screw holes to mark the drill points on the wall. It's always a good idea to check for cables or pipework before drilling into a wall – you can buy battery-operated detectors really cheaply. Drill your holes and put the rawl plugs into the wall (I use 'all-purpose' or 'universal' rawl plugs, which are suitable for all types of wall). I always drill holes for rawl plugs using a drill bit smaller than the rawl plug, because it's easier to make the hole bigger if you need – but if a hole is too big, it's a total pain because you need to start again. So I'd drill initially with a 7mm drill bit. Try to put the rawl plug in – maybe tap it in with a hammer if necessary. If it won't go in, go up to a 7.5mm drill bit. When all four wall holes are ready, place the screws through the holes in the box, guide them into the rawl plugs and screw in place.

 You could paint the boxes the same colour as the wall, or go for a muted complementary colour. Maybe a crazy splash of vibrant colour. Or try painting the inside and outside different colours.

MAGNETIC SPICE-JAR SPACE SAVERS

As in most homes, the space in my kitchen cupboards is pretty limited. One of the things that used to drive me crazy was how much space little spice pots take up because they won't stack, so although they're small they end up on a massive land grab of premium territory. My one small cupboard for tins and jars was a higgledy-piggledy nightmare of stuff that may as well have not been there because I could never see what was lurking.

To maximise the cupboard space, I decided to use the back of the cupboard door. A little, but life-changing, move. The result was not only a much clearer cupboard, but also an unexpected boon in that I use my spices all the time now because they're right there under my nose every time I open the door. I end up thinking 'ooh, I wonder what this would be like if I added that...', so my cooking's got tastier, too! You do need to buy a few supplies for making this, so it's not the cheapest option. But once it's done, you'll love it forever.

you will need

A piece of magnetic stainless steel – to fix to the back of the door, so measure the area you want to cover

Double-sided tape

Strong glass-to-metal glue – to fix the magnets to the jars

Strong magnets

Shallow jars

Embossing label maker (optional)

Method

1 You can find suppliers of magnetic stainless steel very easily online ('magnetic stainless steel cut to size' in the search engine should throw up lots of options). Most of the cost is for the hassle factor of the supplier having to set the machine to cut to size. But once the machine is set and you've paid the premium for one piece, most suppliers should happily churn out as many more as you like for a fraction of the cost of the first, so it's worth considering buying more if you've got other cupboards it will fit. Think – more magnetic jars or a handy place to keep 'to do' lists and shopping lists out of sight but not out of mind...

2 Obviously, you don't want to encroach too deep into the cupboard when the doors are shut, so you need shallow jars for the spice pots. As a rule, I hate buying something I could get for free, like glass jars. But as there's nothing I buy regularly that provides me with a source of squat jars to use for this, I bought some 115g (4oz) short, round jars from an online jam-jar supplier. They're not expensive and it does mean all jars are the same size, with plain silver lids, so they look smart, too.

3 As with most things, I buy the magnets online – a search for '1mm x 10mm disc magnets' should throw up plenty of options. They will cost around £5.00 for 20 and you will need four magnets per jar.

4 Stick the steel to the back of the cupboard door using double-sided tape and the strong glue. The double-sided tape saves you holding it in place while the glue sets.

5 Make the jars by gluing the magnets onto the base of the glass. As the base of the jars is concave, the best way to fix the magnets is to glue four of them, evenly spaced around the rim of the base of each jar. Leave to set.

6 Meanwhile, make labels for the jar lids to identify the contents. If you don't have one, I would say an embossing label maker is a really worthwhile investment. They're not expensive and can be used again and again. Otherwise, handwritten sticky labels will do. Once the glue is set, decant spices into the jars and enjoy!

WHITEWASHED WOOD OFFCUT CHOPPING BOARDS

A chunky wooden chopping board is such a satisfying, practical and easy make. It will cost very little, take marginally more effort and you'll end up with a thing of beauty that will last forever. Chopping boards are another example of something so, so simple that inexplicably cost way more to buy than they really should.

Sources of wood offcuts are timber yards, carpenters and joinery companies. Timber yards tend to sell offcuts. If you make friends with a local carpenter or joiner, they might give you their leftovers for free. Sand the wood to smooth it and round off sharp corners and edges. Clean the board well and leave it to dry. You could leave the board plain and just season with butcher's block oil. But if you want to make a stylish painted finish on the back, it's very simple. Here's how...

Method

❶ Leave one side of the board unsanded so that the paint wash will soak into the grain well. Mix equal quantities of water and emulsion paint and stir well. The wash should have the consistency of milk.

❷ Put a strip of masking tape around the sides of the board so that you don't go over the edges with the paint. Only the back of the board will be painted and you want to make sure you get good clean lines. Dip a slightly damp cloth into the paint wash and rub it over the wood. Only use a little paint and rub the cloth in the direction of the grain, that is, only up and down, not side to side as well, or it will look messy. Paint a couple of thin washes of colour.

❸ Now trace the heart or star template onto a piece of cardboard (see pages 152 and 153 for templates). Cut out the shape using a sharp lino cutter or craft knife to make a stencil.

❹ Place the stencil where you want on the board. Choose a different paint (not watered down) for the heart or star. Make sure it is either darker or lighter than the paint wash, so that it stands out. Apply the paint lightly with a damp sponge. If there is too much paint, it will leach under the lines of the stencil, so less is better. You can always add more if necessary. Dab the sponge over the cut-out to make the design. When you take away the stencil, if paint has spread, clean it away using a cotton bud dipped in a little white spirit. Don't worry about wiping away the wash around the edges of the stencilled design – that will be fixed later.

❺ Leave the paint to dry completely. Go over the board with another wash of thinned paint using the damp cloth. This will cover up any bare patches where you've cleaned up the edges of the stencilled design, if there are any. Also, this blurs the edges of the stencilled design a little, giving a softer, slightly aged look. Again, leave to dry.

❻ Finally, use a soft dry cloth to oil the entire board with butcher's block oil. Rub in two or three thin coats of oil. This prevents the wood from drying out and cracking and also gives the paint a protective coat. That said, you need to take a little care with the painted side so that it doesn't get ruined – obviously, it's not a surface for cutting on! These boards look fabulous on the side in the kitchen – chopping boards you won't want to hide away!

TIP

To clean a wooden chopping board, scrub it with bicarbonate of soda and lemon juice. This will get rid of bad smells and stains. Coiled metal scourers will give you extra muscle if the board's in need of a really good clean. On sunny days put the board in the sunshine, which will dry and bleach it naturally at the same time. Don't forget to oil it occasionally, to stop the wood drying out and splitting.

IRONING BOARD COVER

The ironing board is one of the long list of items around the house that you need to have, but is pretty un-lovely. If you've got space, you can hide it away in a cupboard. If not, it'll be leant against a wall, or hung on the back of a door, ugly but essential. Having got sick of the sight of the cover festooned with burn marks on my board, I decided it was time for a quick fix.

Method

1 Your board is the template, so lay it down on a piece of fabric and draw a line around the perimeter, 15cm away from the edge of the board. Cut the fabric with pinking shears to prevent fraying.

2 Fold over a 4cm-wide hem and pin all the way round. Where the shape is curved, you can cut little snips into the hem to help it gather and fold more easily. Don't worry about being too neat. The hem will be under the board, so it won't be seen. Position the pins perpendicular to the edge of the fabric – that way the sewing machine needle can whizz over them, so you don't have to remove them as you go.

3 Sew around the hem, leaving a 3cm gap between the start and finish of the stitching.

4 Use a safety pin or a bodkin (see page 104) to thread a piece of cord, string or elastic through the hemmed channel. Finally, place the cover on top of the board and pull the ends of the cord tight, so that it gathers and fits securely around the underside of the board. Tie a double bow to fix it. You can easily undo the bow if you need to remove the cover and wash it at some stage.

A small thing, not top of the priority list, but it might help to make doing the ironing marginally more appealing next time, which is no small thing.

Clothes peg pegs

A fabulous use for the humble wooden peg that elevates it to a practical style feature. A row of these looks fantastic – and is so practical.

you will need

Wooden clothes pegs
Small paintbrushes
Emulsion paint
Extra-strong glue

Simply paint the pegs. Use emulsion because a peg is slightly fiddly to paint and you'll get it all over your fingers, so it's miles easier to clean up if you just use a basic water-based paint. Paint the insides of the peg first by pinching it together, then paint the rest, leaving one of the long sides unpainted because you won't see it, as it will be fixed to the wall. Stand the pegs upright and leave to dry for ten minutes or so, then apply another coat. When the paint is dry, make sure the bottoms of the pegs haven't stuck together. Squeeze the tops together to force them apart if they have. Now glue the pegs to the wall using a really strong adhesive. Leave the glue to set properly before putting any weight on your pegs. They should be strong enough to hold anything from tea-towels to coats.

A little health warning: These are so handy and easy to make, before you know it you might end up with a little colony springing up around the house...

★★★ TREE BRANCH PEGS

These are fall-in-love gorgeous. I know, I know, it's a peg, but trust me, there is something about the process of hunting for the perfect stick, gathering it, taking it home, carving it and then hanging your trophy up on the wall that makes it so much more than just a peg.

There is literally no other way I would rather spend a Sunday afternoon than out walking with my family. I don't mean some sort of brisk route march. I mean ambling along, sniffing the air, looking, just being. Whether it's meandering through fields, a park, public gardens, a wood, a beach, one of the finest parts is collecting treasure. Most finds need no embellishment and end up dotted around the house, on shelves, the mantelpiece and window ledges. But sticks offer up a myriad of possibilities and this project is one of my favourites.

you will need

Suitable branches

Saw

Tape measure

Sandpaper, medium grade

Drill with various drill bits ranging from really small up to and including a 4mm drill bit

1 x 7cm screw per peg

1 x size 8 rawl plug per peg

Method

❶ First of all you need to find a branch. About 2cm diameter is a good size. That's about the minimum thickness you want for a good, sturdy hook, but you could go thicker if you prefer. Just look out for long, straight broken branches and snaffle one you like the look of (the pegs I've made here are from a fallen branch of a eucalyptus tree). If the wood is at all damp, leave it to dry out at home for a few days.

❷ Saw straight through the branch to make a flat end for your peg, then measure 11cm from the flat end and make a pencil mark on the underside of the stick. Measure 9cm from the flat end and make a pencil mark on the top side. Basically, you want to carve a gradient spanning 2cm of wood, so that when the slanted edge of the wood is placed against a wall, the stick angles up in the air, creating a peg. Cut into the wood along this gradient, gently rocking the saw at first, so that it goes in at the angle you want, then saw all the way through.

❸ Sand the cut flat end of the wood to smooth and remove the saw marks. It will bring out the rings of the wood, which looks so beautiful in this simple, natural state. Sand the sloped end to smooth it off if it's rough around the edges.

❹ Now you need to drill a hole through the sloped end so that you can screw the peg onto the wall. Make a pencil mark in the centre of the cut oval. The hole has to go straight through from that point to the longer underside of the peg – that is, at a 90° angle. Don't worry about getting out a protractor – it doesn't have to be that exact. Just hold something straight such as a pencil or a ruler against the cut edge so you can see the line the drill needs to follow and mark a pencil dot on the underside of the wood. Hold up the wood so that you can see both pencil dots, position the drill on the mark on the cut end and drill through. The easiest way to make the hole is by starting with a really small drill bit, which will cut right through the wood in a flash, and then drill through the hole a couple more times, increasing the size of the drill bit each time to enlarge the hole. The final drill bit size should be 4mm.

❺ Now your peg's ready to hang. Use 7cm long screws and size 8 rawl plugs to screw it onto the wall (see page 32 for detailed instructions on drilling).

TIP

If the saw is stiff and
dragging, rub oil – any is
fine – over the teeth of the
blade. Now it should work
like the proverbial knife
through butter... well,
maybe with a bit more
elbow grease.

TENNIS BALL DOOR BLOCK

Sometimes you have to have something fixed on the wall behind a door to stop the door just short of smashing into the wall whenever it's thrown open. It's a small thing, but it does a big job, particularly if you've got something hanging on the wall that needs to be protected, or something protruding from it that might damage the door. My issue on this front is that, as with a lot of the little unexciting things, no design thought ever goes into them, so the ones you can buy are pretty ugly. I know they're only little but, still, I hate spending money on something unless I love it or have no alternative. So here's my stylish, practically free alternative.

Half a tennis ball glued to the wall makes the perfect door stop. Because it's made of rubber, it gives a gentle bounce-back to the door when it's been thrown open over-zealously.

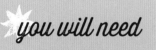

you will need

Tennis ball

Craft knife

Double-sided tape

Some fabric – pretty or plain, but a scrap large enough to cover the outside of the ball, with extra to tuck inside the curve of the ball

Staple gun

Pencil

Extra-strong glue

Method

❶ First, cut the ball in half. Pierce it with a craft knife and then push the knife all the way around the ball to slice it into two. Now cover the outside of one half with double-sided tape. Stick a strip around the inside rim of the ball, too.

❷ Get your fabric and press it onto the tape on the outside of the ball. Stretch the fabric so that it is smooth across the outside. Pull the edges into the inside of the ball and fix them to the tape. If the colour of the ball shows through the fabric, cover with a second layer. To make sure the fabric will hold tight (which is important because if it pulls away, the ball will loosen on the wall), staple the raw ends to the inside of the ball. If the staples in your gun are large and cut though the fabric on the outside, just knock them back a little with a hammer.

❸ To work out where your ball needs to sit on the wall or skirting board so that it stops the door at the right angle, put a large strip of double-sided tape across the back of the ball. Press it lightly onto the wall where you think it should go and just test if the position is right. If not, move it closer to the hinges, or further away, until you find the right spot. Make a little pencil mark underneath so you don't forget where the door block needs to go.

❹ Finally, spread extra-strong glue around the flat rim of the ball and fix it to the wall or skirting board. Grab something big and heavy such as a box or a pile of books that you can press against the tennis ball to hold it in place while it dries. Make sure it is pressing the ball firmly to the wall so the glue gets a good fix. If glue is squelching out around the edges, scrape it away with something like a knitting needle or a knife.

No more wincing every time the door's flung open.

Beach treasure doorstop

Bringing home beach treasure is one of my favourite mementoes of a holiday. These special pieces can trigger a memory as effectively as a scent can take you back to a moment you'd forgotten about. A large heart-shaped grey rock spotted on a beach by my then two-year-old first daughter in Clovelly in Cornwall – I don't think I'd remember the detail of that day so clearly if I didn't have this little anchor sitting on a shelf to help me drift back to it. Similarly, our front doorstop is a large stone picked up on a beach. Just one thing: if you have a wooden floor, stick some felt to the underside to stop it scraping.

Beach treasure pulls

Next time you're on a beach, also keep an eye out for treasure with holes in, which provide a natural, ready-made pull that can be easily attached to the end of a blind or light string. Once you start to look, it's surprising how many pieces you will find. If you find a shell, a soft stone or a piece of coral you like that doesn't have a hole, you can easily drill through it. Just don't try to drill through a hard stone – that won't work.

TASSEL PULLS

There's something very pleasing about making these because they are so quick and easy to produce, you can make them in exactly the colours you like (we've used contrasting colours here to highlight the different sections) and they look so much nicer and funkier than anything you can buy. As you've probably spotted, I generally go for simple, pared-down style. That said, I do like a little bit of fuss occasionally, to soften my natural tendency towards the austere and these little tassels hit the spot.

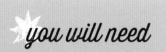

you will need

Strips of fabric, string, embroidery thread, wool or cotton

Scissors

TIP

To make over-sized tassels, wind the thread around something wider than your hand, such as a paperback book.

If you want to make these with fabric, the best material to use is thin cotton, so that you can easily tear it into thin strips. Cutting in a straight line can be tricky, particularly when you just want narrow ribbon-like strips of fabric. By far the quickest, easiest and neatest way to get perfect strips is to rip the fabric apart. See the 'how to' TIP on page 81.

Method

1 This simple method of tassel making just requires winding whatever you're using around your fingers to make a giant loop. Wind it around your hand anywhere between 40 and 80 times, depending on how chunky you want the tassel to be.

2 To make a hanging loop for attaching onto keys, drawers, doors or anything else, take another length (12cm–15cm, depending on how long you want the loop to be) of the same thread or material and tie together to make a loop the length you want it, with several knots on top of each other. You want a chunky ball of knots, to anchor the loop in place.

3 Push the ball of knots through the centre of the top of the string or fabric that's been wrapped around your fingers, so that it is inside the long loops.

4 Take another length of thread and pass it under the folded top end of the loop. Wind it up and over the folded top of the tassel several times, going either side of the hanging loop, to secure it in place. Knot securely.

5 Cut another length of thread and wind it around the tassel several times, about 1cm from the top. This makes the ball shape at the top of the tassel. Knot securely and leave the loose ends hanging.

6 Cut through the bottom end of the tassel, which is still looped. Ruffle the threads around, so that the knotted ball (which is the base of the hanging loop) is hidden inside the tassel. Finally, trim the ends so they are all the same length.

If you are using the tassels as pulls, instead of making a separate hanging loop, make several knots in the bottom of the blind or light cord and push that into the centre of the tassel. These look super smart as cord pulls, but I would suggest you pull on the cord rather than the tassel.

FOAMING PUMP DISPENSER

In my book *Simply Wonderwoman* I mentioned how brilliant foaming pump dispensers are, because they turn any liquid soap or shampoo into foam. All you do is put a little soap in the bottle, top it up with water and it magically converts to foam. It is so much more economical – one bottle of liquid soap lasts about ten times as long this way. Lots of people got in touch to ask where to get them from but, as it can be difficult to find stylish versions to buy, here is a brilliant and practically free option...

...re-styling and reusing pumps that come as part of a manufactured product. I always think of the packaging as a free gift that comes with whatever I'm buying. Glass jars, spray bottles, squeezy bottles, shoe boxes, match boxes... add a little bit of creativity and you can turn an everyday basic into something really very lovely. If your supermarket doesn't sell foaming products, just do an online search for 'foaming handwash'.

you will need

Foaming pump dispenser

Double-sided tape

Scrap of material – big enough to more than cover the body of the dispenser, that is, up to the bit that screws off with the pump. Don't cut the fabric to size at this stage – it's a wasted effort as there is no need.

Fabric scissors

Craft knife

Label maker (optional)

Method

1 Make sure the outside of the dispenser is clean and dry, with any labels removed. White spirit will get rid of any sticky residue. Just wash it away with detergent to get rid of the smell.

2 Completely cover the body of the dispenser with double-sided tape. If it's an odd shape you might need to criss-cross the tape a bit. Don't worry about being neat, but do make sure the entire thing is covered. Peel off the tape backing so the whole bottle is sticky.

3 Carefully wrap the fabric around the bottle so that it is covered. There's no need to try to match up the top and bottom of the bottle with the edges of the fabric. Where the fabric meets at the side of the bottle, bring the underside edges together, so that they are buttressed up against each other, creating a straight line running down the side of the bottle, like a seam. Use fabric scissors to cut away the excess fabric along this 'seam'. Cut away the excess fabric around the bottom of the bottle, too. Finally, use a craft knife to cut away the excess fabric at the top of the bottle, holding the fabric taut and pressing the blade into the gap between the bottle and the screw top. Be careful not to cut into the plastic with the blade.

4 If you have a label maker, stick on embossed or printed plastic strips saying 'wash', 'scrub up', 'shampoo' – whatever's appropriate or whatever you like, or just leave the bottle as it is.

5 Quarter fill the bottle with liquid soap or shampoo and top up with water. Ta da – the life of a bottle of shampoo or liquid soap is multiplied many times over, and the dispenser looks fabulously stylish, too. I decant everything into recovered pump dispensers (foaming or not) – shampoo, conditioner, body oil, washing-up liquid, hand soap... They look great and cost almost nothing. If the fabric gets dirty, wash it clean with a little liquid soap and scrub under running water.

PHOTO KEY BOX

I love practical, life-changing makes. You know how when you do something and it changes the feel of a room or makes your life so much easier? A key box? Doesn't sound that exciting. Life-changing? Well, yes! Giving your keys a home where you can stash and retrieve them in an instant is pretty good for stress levels. How many times do you find yourself running around, late, unable to remember where you put your keys?

you will need

3-bottle wine crate with a sliding lid – wine merchants sell these pretty cheaply as gift packaging. Either check your local wine store, or else look online (put '3-bottle wine box with sliding lid' into the search engine and shop around because prices can vary quite a lot)

Paint – emulsion or eggshell (optional)

Roller and small paintbrush

Drill with 3mm drill bit

Bradawl

8 x 1.2mm x 17mm screw hooks

Photograph or images for the front

Spray acrylic sealant (optional, see method)

Double-sided tape

Size 7 rawl plugs

5cm long screws

Method

1 First, remove the rope handle from the crate, if it has one. Now you can either leave the unfinished pale wood as it is or paint it using a roller and brush. You only need to paint the outside edges of the box and the narrow band that goes around the sliding door. Paint the insides too, if you want. There's no need to paint the sliding door as it will be covered.

2 If you're going to hang your box on the wall, drill four small holes in the corners of the back of the box for screwing it onto the wall. Mark drill points 4cm from the edges.

3 Use a pencil to mark evenly spaced dots where the screw hooks should go. Position a row of three hooks, then a row of two, then another row of three, and stagger the hooks so that the keys don't bunch on top of each other. Pierce each hole using a bradawl and screw in the hooks. The back of the box is made of thin wood, so screw the hooks through until the points are just poking through the back. In other words, don't screw them in as far as you can, because they will stick out at the back too far. Don't worry: it will still be sturdy enough for keys.

4 Choose a photograph to go on the front – a picture or any image you like. Measure the size of the sliding cover exactly (excluding the bit that slides into the grooves of the box) so you know what size image you need. If you can print to fit at home, perfect. If not, order a print online or in a photographic shop. Alternatively, you can print out various images and put them together as a montage. Whatever you are using, the print must have a sealed finish to stop it getting damaged by handprints when the door is open and shut. Photographic printers can use a professional matt heat-treated acrylic sealant. Alternatively, you can buy spray acrylic sealant to apply at home.

5 Stick the image – or images – onto the sliding cover using double-sided tape.

6 If the box is going on the wall, mark drill points on the wall by holding it up and poking a pencil through the screw holes. Fix rawl plugs and screw it on or sit it on a shelf or side. This makes a lovely gift too.

{ The beauty of this is that it doesn't look like
a key box, so you can put it anywhere you
like and it's not a security issue. }

PHOTO BOX

This photo box is a great place to store hard copies of photographs without having to find the time to stick them in an album. How often do you snap away on your camera or phone, upload the pictures to your computer (or don't) and then forget all about them? Spending a few hours every now and then going through the files can be an absolute joy. At the most prosaic level, deleting the rubbish clears space on your computer. Woohoo. But a printed picture is so much more satisfying, as it reminds you of precious moments you can't believe you'd forgotten.

Printing photos is a habit many of us have got out of, because we don't need to get the pictures printed to see what they look like. Remember the days of waiting for your printed roll to come back, then having to bin half of the snaps anyway because heads were cut off or eyes were closed? There is still something very satisfying about having a tangible copy of a memory to flick through occasionally, not just on a computer. Of course, some pictures get framed and proudly displayed, but so many more stay in digital limbo.

you will need

Selection of photos or images

Glue

3-bottle wine crate with a sliding lid, or any box that you can easily get hold of

Spray acrylic sealant

Paint, roller and small paintbrush (optional)

Method

1 Print out a single image or several to cover the lid. Be creative with scale – mixing different-sized images looks funky.

2 Stick your pictures onto the sliding lid, making sure the edges of the prints are stuck down firmly. Cut to size or overlap, whichever you prefer.

3 Protect the images with a coat of acrylic sealant.

4 Cover, paint or leave the rest of the box – as you like.

GIFT IDEAS

This box makes a lovely gift, too, in which case, you might like to add a personal (handwritten or stamped) message or quote inside the box.

Wedding gift: This makes a great wedding present, using pictures from the big day, with a quote inside along the lines of 'It had to be you' (Frank Sinatra).

Valentines Day gift: Try using a mix of photographs spanning a relationship with a quote like 'Have I told you lately' (Van Morrison).

Birth gift: Select some gorgeous baby pictures with a message such as 'How wonderful life is now you're in the world' (Elton John), or 'May your heart always be joyful' (Bob Dylan).

You get the drift. Use a quote that is personal to you, or a heartfelt message, or nothing – just let the pictures speak for themselves.

CROSS-BODY UTILITY SACK

This ultra-useful bag is indispensable inside and outside the home. It's roomy enough to use as a laundry bag, but streamlined enough to carry around, slung across your body as a chic shopping bag. The sizes I have given here are a guide. You can make this lovely bag bigger or smaller, depending on what you want to use it for. It is just a brilliantly easy to make, practical style.

I love making bags for myself and to give as presents because they are so easy and satisfying to whip up. This one can be made unlined, or using the origami-style method of lining described for the purse on page 84 (leave out the zip). Mix and match the fabrics for a pretty, reversible bag.

you will need

2 pieces of fabric – 1 measuring 1m x 40cm (to make the bag); the other, 1m x 16cm (to make the strap), cut with pinking shears, if you have some, to keep the edges of the fabric neat and stop them fraying

Sewing machine and thread

Pins

Method

❶ Fold the big piece of fabric in half lengthways with the right side facing in and sew down each side, 1cm in from the edge. Use the smallest stitch setting on your machine to create a really strong edge. If you prefer to use a bigger stitch, sew a double row for reinforcement.

❷ Make a 2cm-deep hem along the top of the bag, by folding the fabric over twice, so that the raw edges are inside the hem. Pin the hem, placing the pins perpendicular to the edge of the fabric, so the machine needle can whizz over them without breaking, and machine stitch. Turn the bag the right way out.

❸ Now make the strap by folding the long strip of fabric in half lengthways with the right sides facing in. Sew around one short side and the long edge with a 1cm seam allowance, using a short stitch for strength. Turn it inside out using the method for how to make a fabric strap shown on page 80. Fold in the raw edges and machine stitch together.

❹ Sew one end of the strap to the inside edge of the top hem of the bag on one side, right next to the side seam. To keep it neat, sew over the stitching. Reinforce the strap by oversewing a rectangle of stitches, crossed over in the centre.

❺ Pull the strap over to the opposite side of the bag, making sure it is untwisted, and sew it into the inside edge of the top hem diagonally opposite.

These are great hanging on the back of a door to stash anything from laundry to bathroom essentials to cleaning kit. Out and about they're great for carrying books, shopping, picnics, sports kit... the list goes on. They make great gifts, too.

OVERSIZED OILCLOTH SHOPPING BAG

This gorgeous bag is a stylish and practical alternative to plastic supermarket bags, which we know we shouldn't really use anyway.

As is often the case with 'green' alternatives, there's another less ethical reason for embracing the alternative – it can actually make your own life easier. No more thin plastic pulled taut across your hand, biting into it like cheese wire, as you lug your shopping home. No more packing and unpacking loads of small bags. Plus, these look great. And, of course, you get the smug satisfaction of knowing you're doing the right thing. This bag is brilliant for shopping, the beach, picnics, sport, travelling... and I bet you'll be asked where you got it from!

you will need

Sewing machine and thread

1m oilcloth

3.5m 50mm synthetic webbing

Fabric scissors

Double-sided tape

Cut three pieces of oilcloth:

***One long piece, measuring 112cm x 34cm**

***Two shorter pieces, each measuring 41cm x 34cm**

Method

1 Set the sewing machine one notch along from its shortest stitch setting, so the stitches will be tight and strong.

2 Lie the large panel of oilcloth with the right side facing up and the short edge at the top. Position one of the smaller pieces of oilcloth on top with the right side facing down, so that the top edges of the pieces are completely aligned, that is, the 34cm edges are aligned. Sew along the right-hand edge with a 1cm seam allowance, starting right at the top, but finishing 1cm from the bottom of the shorter piece (to allow the base of the bag to be attached). If you want a guide for the seam, draw a pencil line with a ruler.

3 It is important to finish loose ends well, to make sure the bag is strong. Weave the ends in and out of the stitches along the seam for about 2cm and then knot again several times.

4 Now turn the long piece of oilcloth around 180° and place the second shorter piece on top with the right side facing down, again making sure the 34cm-long edges of the pieces are completely aligned. Sew along the right-hand edge with a 1cm seam allowance, and stopping 1cm short from the bottom of the shorter piece.

5 With the oilcloth lying right side up, open it up to form an s-shape. Fold the long central piece up into a u-shape (the right sides will be facing in). Make the folds in line with the 41cm sides of the smaller oilcloth pieces. Fold in the side flaps to complete the sides of the bag. Align the top edges and sew down each side seam. Finally, sew together the seams on the base of the bag. Flip the bag the right way out and push out the corners.

6 Now cut two pieces of webbing for the handles, each measuring 175cm. The easiest way to position the webbing is to hold it in place using small pieces of double-sided tape dotted down the centre of the webbing. Be careful not to put tape where the stitches will go, because when the needle zips in and out it will get sticky residue on it, which will slow it down and make the thread snap. Position the webbing about 4cm in from each side seam. Start by fixing one end to the centre of the underside of the bag, loop around the top and finish by joining the two ends on the bottom, overlapping the webbing by 2cm. Fold the end over by 2cm so it doesn't fray. The handles should be about 64cm long.

TIP

To get perfect right angles when cutting fabric, use a large book or magazine to make sure the corners are right angles. Place a metre rule along the edge of the book to ensure the line is straight, and mark the length you need. The beauty of using oilcloth is that the pieces effectively stick together when faced right side in for sewing, so there is no need for pinning. Also, the edges won't fray, so there is no need for hemming either.

Homemade giving is about pleasure – for you and the receiver. In our busy lives, giving can sometimes become a chore as we panic at the last minute about what to get. A little bit of thought ahead of time turns it back to the thoughtful, enjoyable process it is meant to be. And by opting to make something yourself – or at least include an element of homemade – you can make a gift really personal. It also shows you have taken time over what you're giving, which is often cherished above the gift itself. Isn't it great when you're so excited about the present you're giving that you can't wait for someone to open it?

Many of these makes can be done in minutes, but some take longer, such as knitting. As with cooking a nice meal, whatever you're going to do, think ahead a little to make sure you've got the right ingredients, which includes some time to set aside. What you don't want to do is find yourself stressing at the last minute that you've added something into the daily mix that you don't have time for.

Some of the best presents that go on giving the longest are the simplest things. A book, a hand-picked collection of songs, a box set or a movie, a meal, a photograph. All of my homemade gifts are about simple pleasures, whether it's the comfort of a hand-knitted scarf on a cold night or the scent and glow of a homemade candle, a picnic on a personalised blanket, breakfast in bed or some delicious homemade chocolate honeycomb with a cup of tea.

And, of course, the added bonus of homemade giving is that it's so much more pleasurable to take a little time being creative at home, rather than bustling round the shops. Time to breathe…

CLAY TEA LIGHT SHADES

I absolutely love these pretty tea light shades, because they look so stylish, but take just minutes to make and really couldn't be easier to produce.

you will need

White air-dry clay – I always buy it online for ease, but craft shops stock it

Ruler

Stamps – use lace, fabric, Indian print blocks, or anything that will leave an imprint

Rolling pin

Sharp knife

Tea lights

Method

1. Break off a fist-sized chunk of the clay and roll it out into a rough rectangle that is about 2mm thick. Your final cut shape should be about 22cm x 5cm, so make sure you roll out a piece bigger than that.

2. Imprint the clay with your chosen stamp to leave a pattern on the surface of the clay. If you are using lace, use the rolling pin to press it into the clay so that it leaves a strong imprint. Think creatively about what you might use. I also use Indian print blocks or fabric with a chunky weave. The side of a tin can give a nice ribbed pattern. Or dot holes along the length, randomly, or in a pattern or shape.

3. Neaten up the rectangle by cutting it out with a sharp knife. Shape one end to a point, like a belt. Gently pick up the clay and wrap it round, with the pattern on the outside, so that it forms a tube, with the pointed end overlapping on the outside. Softly but firmly press the overlapped pieces together so that they fix and hold. Stand the pot and gently shape again, so that the base and top are as round as possible. Don't worry that it's not a perfect cylinder. Part of the appeal here is the slightly wibbly, organic look that underlines that this is homemade – with love – not churned out on a production line. Now just leave the clay to air dry. It will dry to a crisp white, like beautiful unfinished porcelain.

4. Light a tea light, position your masterpiece over it and admire. They look best on a shelf where you can't see the tea light inside, just the glow out of the top or through the holes. So pretty.

Although these are fairly robust, they're too delicate to just wrap up and hand over, so if you're giving them as a present, do put them in a little box before wrapping. Package up some tea lights too, in a bag or jar.

SIMPLE CANDLES

I have given up buying good scented candles, as they are so expensive to buy – unless they're massively reduced in a sale. As with most stylish treats the bulk of the expense goes on the packaging and the 'feel-good factor'. I mean, buying something dirt cheap never feels luxurious, does it? Hence, things are often priced high to get you to buy. Crazy! Making candles really couldn't be easier and gives you and the person you're giving it to a much warmer glow – of satisfaction – than a shop-bought one.

★ you will need

Wax – buy by the kilo – 1kg should make around 6–8 good-sized candles. Container wax is preferable as it will not shrink when it sets, whereas wax for non-container candles will pull away from the mould

2 saucepans – 1 larger than the other

Candle perfume (optional)

Suitable containers – small jam jars, teacups, Kilner jars...

Wick – buy by the metre, so you can cut to size. Container candles need a wick with a core, to keep it upright when the wax turns to liquid as it burns. Small, metal-core wick should be perfect for most candles (up to 5cm diameter)

Wick sustainers – little discs of metal with a hole in the middle that support the wick at the base

Wax glue – to fix the sustainers to the base of your container

I was put off making my own candles for a long time because it seemed like a pretty confusing and faffy business (so many permutations and options on what to use). And I hate things that take more effort than the reward reaped. So, I set out to make it simple and couldn't understand why it had taken me so long.

There are various waxes to choose from, so below is a quick explanation of the basic options. Mineral wax is petroleum based – it looks shiny and white when hard. This is what most candles you buy are made of, including a lot of the big-name, ultra-expensive ones. Soy wax – made from soya beans – is quite fashionable because it's 'natural', although, obviously, petroleum is natural, too. But you know what I mean. Soy wax looks dull and off-white when hard. Beeswax is the most natural of all, but it is much more expensive than the others. Or you can very easily melt down and reuse old candles – you know how a pillar candle leaves a hollowed out shape that doesn't burn, or the bottom of a candle in a pot that won't burn down, or any naff old candles that you want to render down and restyle. But don't forget: if you're using wax from non-container candles it might shrink a little. Personally I find mineral container wax easiest to work with.

The easiest way to scent a candle is to buy special candle perfume, which you can get from any candle-making supplier. Just beware, though – a lot of them do smell pretty unnatural. The name on the label's not always a great indicator of what it's going to smell like, so do try to sniff before you buy. I would recommend one you might not opt for, because it sounds a little odd, and that's tomato. It's a bit like fig. If you want something with a bit more punch, add pepper. Again, it sounds strange, but it works. You can use essential oil, but it takes you down the route of extra hassle, as not all essential oils are suitable and it's a faff to work out which are, so I wouldn't bother. And anyway, candle perfume costs about the same or less. ☞

{ **TIP** To work out how much wax you need for your container, fill it with water, then pour it into a measuring jug. The number of millilitres of water is equal to the number of grams of wax you will need. }

Method

1 To make the candle, cut up whatever wax you're using into smallish bits (if it hasn't come in flakes or beads) and place in the small saucepan. Now third fill a bigger saucepan with boiling water. Sit the smaller pan inside the big one – the heat from the water will melt the wax. It is tempting to melt the wax directly over the heat, but it can be dangerous as there's a risk of the wax bursting into flames. Anyway, using two pans is barely any more effort. (Do not use a bowl for the melting wax, as it will get hot and you need a handle for pouring – and a bowl could smash if you accidentally dropped it, sending hot wax flying over your kitchen.) Once the wax is completely melted, turn off the heat. If you've used old candles, don't worry about fishing out any old wicks or residue. The bits will stay in the bottom of the pan when you pour out the wax. Leave the wax to cool for a couple of minutes before adding your scent. Add 5ml of perfumed oil per 100g.

2 While the wax is melting, get your containers ready. I like jam jars for their simplicity – and they're free and have lids. Plant pots and Kilner jars look really stylish, too, but be as creative as you like. Teacups are always popular – although they're a little bit chichi for my taste generally, who doesn't like a dash of pretty kitsch now and then? And they do make really beautiful gifts.

3 Thread the wick through the sustainer. Pull a little of the wick through the bottom of the sustainer and bend it over so it lies flat underneath. Crimp the metal tubing that the wick goes through with a pair of pliers to hold the wick in place. Flatten the metal disc base if it crumples up when you crimp. If you're lazy like me, you can forget the pliers and crimp the wick between your teeth. Use a knife to scrape out a blob of wax glue, spread it onto the underside of the sustainer and fix it to the centre of the inner base of the container. Hold the wick up straight and cut it so that it is 1–2cm higher than the container. The beauty of using metal-core wicks is that they will stand up straight on their own until the wax hardens. If the wick won't stay centred, lie something like a chopstick or a knife over the top of the container to lean the wick against to keep it in position.

4 Once the wax is cool, pour it into your pots. Pour some over the wick as you go, so that it will light easily later. Again, don't worry if any residue from old candles does make it into the pots. It will sink to the bottom of the melted wax, so you won't see it when the candle is hard. If the wax is too hot when it goes into the pot, it might melt the wax glue, so the wick sustainer comes unstuck. If that happens, press it back down onto the base again using a knife or something similar. Leave to set hard – a couple of hours or so.

5 Once the wax is hard, cut the wick short so that it begins about 0.5cm above the wax.

If you've used a jam jar, you might want to finish off your gift by spray painting the lid, or covering it with fabric (fix it on with double-sided tape). If you like, add a label to identify the scent.

When you're cleaning up, remember – don't ever put any wax down the sink. It will get hard and block the drain – doh!! If there's any wax left in the pan, either scrape it out or reheat gently so it melts, then pour it into something to set and be thrown away. White spirit will remove any wax residue from your pots, then clean really well in hot water and washing-up liquid. Baby wipes are brilliant for wiping the wax off any utensils that have wax or wax glue on them.

{ **It will cost about the same to make around eight candles as to buy one posh one. What's not to love?!** }

CANDLE TIPS

● If you have an old candle that's dusty, pour boiling water over it – it washes the grime away in a flash. Hello, new candle! Pour the water into a cup and leave to cool so that liquid wax hardens and can go in the bin, rather than risk blocking the sink.

● Neaten up a candle that's burned unevenly, or has dents in the top, by gently melting the wax using a hairdryer on a low setting. Go carefully so that you don't accidentally blast melted wax out of the container. Leave to set and it will be good as new.

● To stop your fingers getting burned when you're lighting candles, use kitchen tongs to hold the match. Especially brilliant if you're lighting tea lights in tall glass jars.

● Always fish out any bits of broken match or excess wick from a burning candle. If you leave them, they can burn and flare up dangerously when the candle's burning low.

● My favourite ways of wrapping candles for giving are to use either cellophane or fabric bags. A giant roll of cellophane is useful to keep stashed away. It's especially handy for packaging up teacup candles, as it holds them together and protects them. Bring the sides up over the top of the cup and tie the fanned ends of the cellophane with pretty ribbon or string. For all other candles, I make simple gift bags – see page 79.

KNITTING

Knitting. Ah, where do I begin? Therapeutic, calming, just plain satisfying. It's one of those things you don't get until you try it. Then it's like you've been ushered into a secret world of those in the know. Such pleasure from something so simple. A couple of sticks, a ball of wool, curl up... so many possibilities.

I would describe myself as a born-again knitter. I used to do it when I was at school and remember being completely absorbed by it. But then studying took over and my needles were put away and forgotten. It was only after I published my first book and a colleague got in touch to say her sanity-saver is knitting that I thought about taking it up again. I am so glad she mentioned it. Knitting is uber. It is hip. It is easy. And it is portable, so you can do it anywhere. Long journeys flash by as you click away contentedly. On the sofa. The beach. Anywhere. Like those old Martini ads – any time, any place, any where...

As I was very rusty I got a wonderful and very talented friend to come round and give me and the girls a knitting lesson. It's a great way to do it, if you know someone (who is patient!) who can guide you. If not, here's the basic knowledge you'll need to get up and running... 🖝

{ If you're making something big, use big wool and big needles. Anything else will take too long, and no-one likes a projects that outstays its welcome. }

Changing wool

You'll need to do this when your ball of wool runs out, or if you want to change colours. If you can, it is best to change wool at the start or end of a row, so you don't have to worry about accidentally pulling the knot through a stitch. It's not disastrous if you suddenly find you need to change yarn halfway along a row, but try to make sure the knot pulls all the way through the stitches, or it will leave a hole where the wool hasn't pulled tight. Whenever you change wool, leave long (10cm) ends that can be woven in (see right).

Casting on

Make a slip knot in the wool, leaving a tail of about 10cm. Put the loop onto one of the needles and pull it so it is snug. Pick up the needle in your left hand. Hold the loose end of the wool against the needle to keep it out of the way. Hold the other needle in your right hand. Insert the right needle up through the bottom of the stitch on the left needle and to the back of the left needle, making a cross with the needles. Now loop the yarn anticlockwise around the right needle and bring it forwards between the two needles. Hold the yarn firmly against the right needle and gently slide the right needle through the top of the slip knot on the left needle and under towards the front of the left needle, pulling the yarn you wrapped around it through the loop. Transfer the loop onto the left needle and gently pull it tight (but not too tight – the stitches need to be able to slide). That's it! First two stitches cast on. Working into the first stitch (the one nearest the tip) on the left needle, repeat until you've done as many as you need.

Knit stitch

Start exactly as you do with casting on, but when you get to the bit where the right needle passes through the wool that's been wound around, don't pull a loop to place onto the left needle, but keep the loop snugly on the right needle and slip the original stitch off the left needle. When you knit a stitch, the working yarn always stays at the back of the right needle.

Purl stitch

This is effectively a reverse of the knit stitch. With the yarn at the front of the right needle, insert the right needle down through the top of the first stitch on the left needle and to the front, making a cross with the needles. Loop the wool around the back of the right needle, so that it passes through the two needles. Holding the wool firmly against the right needle, and gently slide the right needle down through the bottom of the loop on the left needle and back behind the left needle, pulling the yarn you wrapped around the right needle through the loop. Pull the working yarn tight and slip the original stitch off the left needle. When you purl, the working yarn stays at the front of the right needle. Mixing knit and purl, you can create all sorts of patterns!

Casting off

Knit two stitches onto the right needle. Then use the tip of the left needle to pick up the first stitch on the right needle. Carry this stitch over the second knitted stitch on the righ needle and off the needle. Knit another stitch and repeat, pulling the first stitch over the second one and so on. When you have one stitch remaining on the right needle, just cut the wool to leave a tail of about 10cm. Slip the stitch off the needle and pass the end of the yarn through the last stitch and pull tightly.

Finishing loose ends

When you've got to the end of your knitting, the prospect of tidying up the loose ends seems like a hassle. It's one of those things that is more off-putting than it should be because, actually, it is very easy to do. It's also satisfying because, with very little effort, you can whittle away the ends and make them disappear so it looks like they were never there. Thread the loose end through a darning needle and weave it in and out of the backs of the stitches. The easiest way to do it is to run the needle in and around stitches and then pull the thread through all at once. It's best to weave ends through along the edges of the knitting, but if you have to weave across through the pattern, it's not disastrous. By echoing the stitches you should still be able to make the ends completely disappear.

For a strong finish, pull a needle length through, tie a slip knot, pull another needle length through, knot, pull through a few more stitches and trim. Whether or not you need a strong finish depends on what you're making. I do it on things that need to be hardwearing, such as scarves, but on most other things a length simply woven through should suffice.

Buying wool

A quick word on buying wool: beware – it can be very expensive. I had this idea of only knitting butter-soft beautifully coloured cashmere – until I discovered the crazy cost of buying it. My tip for a great alternative is 100% alpaca, or a mix of fibres, which is just as gorgeous and supersoft, but much better value. It is not cheap buying any good-quality wool, but I would say, if you are taking the time to knit something that will hopefully last forever, it is worth buying the best, softest wool you can afford.

If you are buying in skeins, you'll need to roll it into balls before you start knitting with it, or it will just end up in a tangled, and frustrating, mess of knots. Done that. Trust me, it's a cut corner that wastes a lot more time and effort in the long run. Some shops have a machine to ball wool when you buy it, so don't forget to ask. If you have to do it yourself, the easiest way I've found is to forget getting someone to hold the loops around their arms; just do it yourself with the loops around your ankles. Carefully unwind the twisted skein so that it is one big loop. Either untie or snip the threads holding the strands of wool together. Put your feet up on the sofa and put the loop over your ankles. Stretch out so the wool is taut. Now just unravel at your own pace, winding the wool into a ball as you go.

Before you start

Before you crack on, don't plunge straight into a project. Practise by casting on eight stitches and knitting eight rows a few times. It'll take a little while to get the hang of the tension. It's not difficult, but you just need to get the feel of it. The first couple of rows will always feel stiff, but the tension eases off once you get into your third row, which makes the knitting much easier and smoother. It's also a good idea to keep checking the number of stitches on the needle while you're practising, because it's very easy to accidentally add extra stitches, or drop some, when you're starting out. Stitches get added when you accidentally hook an extra loop when you pass the right-hand needle through the loop on the left, so you just need to watch that carefully at the start.

Happy knitting!

ZEN KNITTING TIP

In the event of a knitting catastrophe – wrong stitches, or the needle slips clean out of the knitting – DON'T PANIC! Stay calm. Lay the knitting flat on a surface and remove both needles. This requires Zen-like calm. Pull the loose end gently to undo the last few rows, or as many as necessary to get you back to the pre-cock-up point. It will reveal a line of perfect loops. Carefully slot one needle through all except the last loop, where the loose end of yarn is. You will see the loose end is between the last stitch and the penultimate one. Put this last stitch on the other needle and knit as though you were finishing the row – this the last stitch. That's it. You can carry on knitting as normal from here. One note: if the needle doesn't slip into a stitch easily on this row, it's because it went back onto the needle the wrong way round. Just hook it off and turn it around before carrying on knitting. Phew. And hurray. I learnt this the hard way.

KILT-PIN SCARF

Scarves are one of the simplest things you can knit and probably the first thing any knitting novice will make. I am a total scarf addict – there's nothing simpler to schuzz up an outfit.

So as I already had a fairly extensive scarf repertoire before I 'refound' Knitting (with a capital K as I'm so evangelical about it!), I wanted to come up with a real basic knit, but equally, something that would look stylish enough to have been found in a funky boutique. Rather than go long, I decided to go shortish and wide, so that rather than being knotted, it could be secured by a pin. This makes for a really cosy, snug neck warmer that looks gorgeous.

you will need

200g chunky yarn – around four or five balls (just check the label for the weight)

8mm/US size 11 needles

Nappy-pin or kilt pin – these are easily found in a haberdashery or online very cheaply. A lovely brooch would work just as well if you prefer

Method

Cast on 42 stitches, which should give you a scarf width of about 38cm. The pattern alternates two knit and two purl stitches on every row. Each row will start and end on a knit stitch, which means the knit and purl stitches alternate on each row to make a really cool, slightly holey pattern that looks a little bit like crochet. It works brilliantly with the chunky wool and chunky needles to create warmth, without bulk. The proper name for this stitch is moss stitch. So, knit two stitches, bring the yarn to the front, purl two stitches, move the yarn to the back and knit, knit, purl, purl your way through your wool. Try the scarf against yourself when you're nearing the end to be sure it's the perfect length. Mine is 140cm long (or 110 rows), which took just over four balls of wool, but clearly there's no need to be prescriptive about number tallies here. Like most things, it can become a bit of a palaver when you have to be too precise.

This scarf isn't super-quick to knit, but it is easy. The final dimensions of the scarf are about 38cm x 140cm, so it's quite a lot of knitting! But, I would say, the joy is in the knitting, and as it is so simple, you can easily put it down and pick it up any time without stressing about a pattern. Every row starts with knit stitches, so no need to remember where you left off. I guarantee that as soon as you've finished this, you'll want to start up again right away with another.

{ If you're giving this scarf as a gift, why not package it up in a simple gift bag (see page 79), with a basic lavender bag, to keep moths at bay when it's not being worn? }

★ ★ ★
KNITTED WRIST WARMERS

As you know by now, I like to keep things simple, and these wrist warmers really couldn't be simpler. They're made from a basic knitted rectangle sewn together, with a gap left in the seam for a thumb hole. They look really cute.

These cosy wrist warmers are perfect for days with a slight chill, but when gloves are too warm and you want your fingers free. You could roll them up and stick them in a beautiful mug for an invitingly cosy gift. Mmmm, where's the hot chocolate?

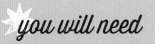

you will need

50g chunky yarn

8mm/US size 11 needles

Darning needle

Method

❶ Cast on 21 stitches. Leave the loose end long – about 20cm – so that you can use it to sew up the seam at the end.

❷ These warmers use the lovely moss stitch pattern, like the kilt-pin scarf (see page 66), but alternating single stitches rather than two. So, knit, purl, knit, purl your way through each row. As there are an odd number of stitches on each row, no need to remember which stitch to start each row with to get the criss-cross effect of moss stitch – it's always a knit stitch. Keep going for 32 rows and then cast off, again leaving a 25cm tail.

❸ You should have a rectangle measuring approx 19cm x 18cm. Fold the rectangle in half. If you fold the 18cm length in half you will have a slightly narrower and tighter glove than folding it the other way – it's up to you which size you want. Now sew up the seams using the loose ends, from top to bottom and bottom to top. Leave a 2cm gap, 6cm from the top, for the thumbhole.

❹ Turn the tube inside out, so that the seam is on the inside.

❺ Repeat steps 1–4 to knit the second wrist warmer.

The boyfriend/ husband/dad scarf

I don't know about you, but I find men pretty difficult to buy for, so clocking the possibilities of knitting for the men in my life was a hallelujah moment. Scarf, e-book reader cover, glasses case cover, another scarf in a different colour...

For a suitably manly scarf, I go for a gorgeous chunky rib.

you will need

300g chunky yarn

9mm/US size 13 needles

Cast on 52 stitches. Like the kilt-pin scarf (see page 66) this involves alternating two knit and two purl stitches on each row. However, to get the rib, you need to start and end each row on a different stitch, so you need the same number of knit and purl pairs of stitches on each row. If you want to scale the number of stitches up or down, the number needs to be even when halved. You could do it with an odd number, but then you need to remember whether you're starting the row on knit or purl each time. Why give yourself the hassle? So, knit, knit, purl, purl, until you've hit about 180cm.

As with any of these homemade presents, this scarf is really easy to make, but does take a bit longer than most. So don't forget to plan this a little in advance, so you don't end up getting stressed trying to finish it.

E-BOOK READER/NOTEBOOK COVER

This practical, stylish gift also includes a great 'how to' tip – how to knit stripes without constantly having to cut and knot the yarn, which results in loose ends everywhere.

I love the sweet simplicity of stripes, but hate the faff of having to keep chopping and changing wool, so naturally had to investigate a super simple way to do it. The added bonus with this project is it is a cover for something small, so you should be able to knit this super-quick.

Method

1 Keep the balls well apart to stop the separate yarns getting tangled, but pull the loose ends together as though they were one strand. Knot a loop of both colours together onto the needle. Effectively, you have two loops, but think of it as one.

2 Using both colours together (as if they were a single strand), cast on 18 stitches. You will see 36 loops, but it represents 18 stitches.

3 Knit the first stitch onto the next row using the two-colour double strand. This brings both colours up to the next row. To ensure a neat end, make sure both of the yarns are pulled snugly.

4 Once you have knitted the first double stitch, choose the colour you want for the first stripe and knit using just the single strand of your chosen colour to the end of the first row. Knit the second row with the same single strand. At the end of the second row, knit the final stitch using both colours to carry the second (redundant for now) colour onto the next (third) row. As before, continue to the end of the row using the single thread in the correct colour. Knit back again to the double stitch and, again, use both colours for the first stitch on the next row. Continue for eight rows to get a nice chunky band of colour. If you want a thinner band, knit four rows. The key thing to remember is that two colours will be knitted together on the first and last stitch of every other row so that you can chop and change colour as you want.

I've used two tonal shades as I love the way the colours meld and blend together, but bright, contrasting colours would look fab too.

5 After eight (or four, if you want narrower bands of colour) rows switch colour. Whichever colour you are knitting with, don't forget to carry both colours up the side, by knitting the first and last stitch double stitches of every two alternate rows with both strands. Always pull those double stitches tight to keep them neat. That edge will be slightly thicker than the rest of the piece, but if you keep the double stitches tight, it won't be obvious.

6 Knit 112 rows. When you cast off, again, use both colours as a double stitch. Casting on and off with both colours means the ends are chunkier which gives a really nice finish.

7 Fold up 15cm from the bottom (make sure whichever side you want to be on the outside is facing in) and sew up the sides, overstitching with wool. Weaving the loose ends into the seams. Flip the pouch inside out.

8 You can secure the pouch either with a tie or a couple of 17mm snap fasteners. The tie's a bit fussier, so I think it's more girly, whereas neat poppers are more masculine. If you're going for the tie, finger knit (see page 77) a 75cm length of both colours together. Keep the loose ends long – 15cm – so that you can use a darning needle to pull them inside the pouch to hide them. Thread the finger-knitted tie through the back of the pouch, in the centre. Pull the stitches to make a hole and push the end of the tie through. Pull it back through another hole 0.5cm along. Make sure the loop is halfway along the tie, then secure it with a slip knot.

8 If you're using the snap fasteners, sew one half of each popper at the corners of the flap (see picture on page 71). Match up the other halves on the pouch and sew in place.

TIPS

The handy thing about having one of these for an e-reader is that you can keep the charger lead in it too, so you've always got it to hand when you need it.

★ ★ ★

If you want to give one of these to someone and don't know if they've got an e-reader – or even if you know they definitely don't have one – slip a notebook and pen inside. It will keep bits together and protect any precious diary, book or photographs from the rough and jumble of an overloaded bag.

★★★ MOBILE PHONE POUCH

This is such a cute little pouch that can be slung around a neck, wrapped around a wrist, looped around a bag strap or hung on a peg. A really neat and sweet way of keeping track of your mobile phone.

Plus it can hold a credit card and cash, and keys can be fixed to it, too (use a karabiner to clip your key ring onto the strap), so there's no need for anything bigger for a walk on the beach, a jog (just plug in the headphones and pin the case to clothes with a big safety pin to stop it bouncing around), walking the dog, or any other quick trip that doesn't require the entire contents of a handbag to be lugged around.

you will need

50g chunky wool

6mm/US size 10 needles

Darning needle

Popper (optional)

Needle and thread (optional)

Method

1 Cast on 16 stitches. Knit each stitch on every row for 140 rows. You should have a rectangle that measures 8cm x 135cm. Finish off the ends (see pages 64–5).

2 Now knit the strap by casting on four stitches – use the same wool or a contrasting one. Knit each stitch on every row for 280 rows. It sounds like a lot, but it's super quick as it's so narrow. You should have a long strip measuring about 1.5cm x 110cm. No need to finish the loose ends, because they will be inside the case.

3 Fold up 12cm of the large rectangle. Run one end of the long knitted strip along the 12cm gap – it will form the sides of the phone pouch, looping up and over to make the neck strap. Anchor the end of the strip to the point where the fold is with a stitch and then sew up each side. Use wool to sew along the edge with an overstitch. To hide loose ends, knot at the top of the pouch and then weave the loose end down into the seam. Once both sides have been sewn, flip the pouch inside out, as you would with stitched fabric.

4 The flap is long enough not to need to be held closed, but if you want, you can sew on a popper using a needle and thread.

This is a lovely project as it's so useful, but so quick and easy to make as it's only little.

GLASSES CASE

This beautiful, soft, ultra-chunky knit will protect glasses from scratches, but it takes up barely any space when it's empty in a bag – unlike hard cases, which are practical but bulky.

This is made using my favourite knitting stitch – moss stitch. I love the contrast of the soft, chunky weave with the industrial-style metal zip.

Method

❶ The extra-thick knit is made by knitting two chunky yarns together, both the same colour. It's a good way to use up the ends of balls. If you don't have two the same colour, just split a ball in two.

❷ Using both strands together, cast on 19 stitches. Double knit (i.e. continuing to use both strands together) alternate stitches – knit, purl, knit, purl and so on, to the end of the row. Repeat on the next row – knit, purl, knit, purl... The reason for casting on an odd number of stitches is so that you can start each row with a knit stitch, so you don't need to remember where you were if you put it down and pick it up again, but it will build up a pattern of staggered stitches, to create the rough weave.

❸ Work 17 rows, then cast off. You should have a 20cm square.

❹ Don't be daunted by the next part – sewing in the zip. It really is easy. Fold the knitted square in half. Open the zip and hand stitch the joined end of it against the fold, to hold it in position. Machine or hand stitch down one side. Repeat with the other half. Keep the zip open.

❺ If you've machine stitched the zip, you may as well carry on and machine stitch around the two open sides of the case, for ease and speed. If not, just hand stitch the seams using yarn or thread. If you do use a machine, just be careful not to let the wool catch on the foot of the machine as you go.

❻ Turn the right side out through the zip so the seams are inside. Make sure the ends of the zip are neat and firmly anchored inside, using extra stitches, if necessary.

You could give this with the glasses strap (see page 77) and use the strap to tie a pretty package together.

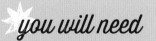

you will need

50g chunky yarn, divided into 2 balls

8mm/US size 11 needles

10cm zip – preferably with metal teeth as they look fab against the wool

Needle and thread

Sewing machine (optional)

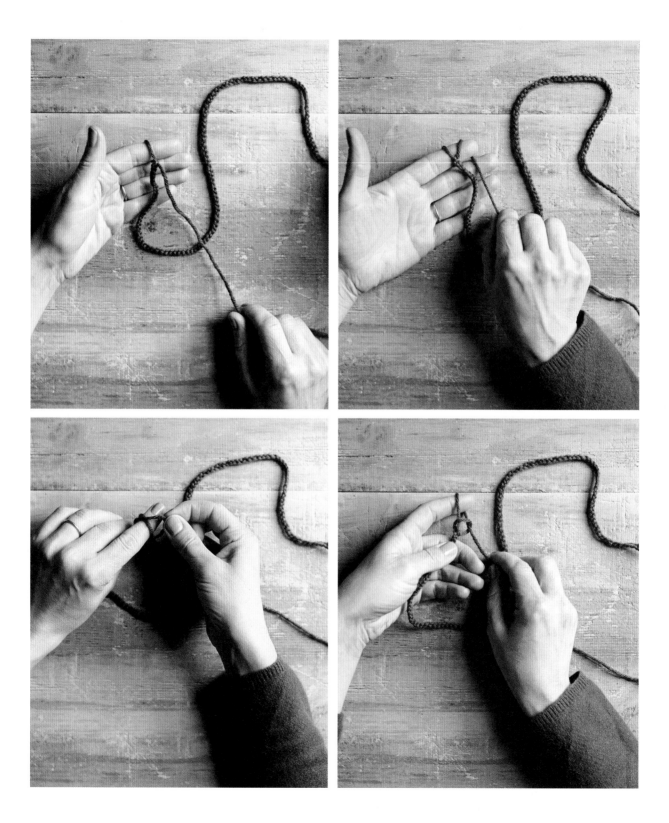

★ GIVING ★

FINGER KNITTING

This is something you may have done in primary school but forgotten all about. I had, until my sister reminded me. We used to make reams of it when we were little. It's satisfying because it's so simple, quick and easy. It is perfect for making straps and ties.

Method

So here's how you do it. Leave a loose end of yarn – about 20cm – then make a large knot loop on the yarn. Put the loop on your forefinger across the first joint right by your fingernail. Pull it snug but not tight. Now pull the loose yarn up and over your finger, closer to the nail, so you have two loops on your finger. Pull the first over the second and off your finger. Pull the knot tight by pulling and wriggling the wool – you'll see what I mean when you do it. This is the reason for leaving a long loose end – you can hold it to pull the knot when you start. Repeat until you have the length you need.

Glasses strap

Here's a simple, sweet little make to hopefully end the interminable refrain of 'where did I put my glasses?' It's so quick and easy to do, it's really a mini gift that can be given any time to anyone who you think might appreciate it. All it is is a length of finger-knitted yarn that can be fixed onto the handles of glasses, a version of those glasses chains you can buy in shops which do the trick but... well... these are cuter.

So, just finger knit an 85cm length. Use any yarn you like – cotton, wool, metallic, thick, thin – they'll all look great. Leave a 10cm length of unknitted yarn at each end to tie onto the glasses handles (if you tie the finger-knitted part around it will be too bulky). The excess is much longer than you need, but will make it easy to tie a knot to fix around the arms of the glasses. Just cut away the extra length.

A lanyard for house keys

Finger knit an 85cm length as above, but knot the ends together. It can be slipped onto a key ring for someone who's always losing their keys...

TIP If you need to put down your finger knitting before its finished, slip the loop over a pencil to hold it and stop your finger knitting unravelling.

SIMPLE GIFT BAG

As long as you have a sewing machine, these are almost as quick to make as cutting out a piece of paper and wrapping a parcel. Actually, I reckon in a challenge I could do this faster than paper wrapping. Anyway, the point is that they are super quick and easy, but they look great.

You can make these sweet little bags with any scraps of cheap fabric. As you don't need much material you can also use offcuts of expensive fabrics, like a Liberty print, without having to spend a fortune.

Method

Cut or tear two squares of fabric (see the 'how to' on tearing fabric on page 81). Align the two pieces, then machine stitch around three sides. If you like the edges raw, you can leave them on the outside. If you prefer a more finished look, flip the bag inside out so that the edges are inside. Obviously, you need to sew with the right sides of the fabric faced accordingly. Again, leave the top edges unfinished if you like, or zip around to make a quick hem if you prefer. Tie with a strip of fabric or ribbon. To make a simple drawstring bag, cut a small hole in the top hem and thread ribbon through (see page 104 for a tip on threading a ribbon), then tie the ends together. So pretty.

The simplest lavender bag

Just grab any scraps of fabric you have – enough for both sides to be the same, or mismatched looks sweet, too. Cut two equal squares, either by folding the fabric in half with the right side facing out, or placing the pieces of fabric on top of each other with the right sides facing out. Cut the fabric with pinking shears, to stop the edges fraying. Whizz around three sides using a sewing machine. Fill with lavender and sew up the opening. Done in 60 seconds (or so).

{ So much more eco-friendly than wrapping paper that gets thrown away. These bags can be used forever. }

BOTTLE GIFT BAG

Giving a bottle of something lovely is always a welcome gift, but it can feel a little impersonal, so here's a nice way of adding a personal touch – a fabric bottle bag.

A magnum of wine makes a great present as it's slightly unusual and looks vastly more expensive than it is, unless you're buying a ridiculously expensive wine of course. Basically it's exactly the same price as buying two bottles of wine (which it is by volume) but it looks far more impressive.

you will need

Bottle

About ¼ m pretty fabric (or felted wool if you want to make a slightly sturdy holder that will give some protection to the bottle)

Fabric scissors

Sewing machine and thread

Pins

Ribbon, string or fabric strip – to use as a tie

Method

1 Place the bottom of the bottle on the fabric and use it as a template – draw and cut out a circle 4cm wider than the bottle itself. Next, roll the fabric around the bottle and cut out a rectangle 5cm wider and higher than the area that would neatly cover the bottle.

2 Fold the rectangle in half lengthways to make a tube with the right side facing in and sew a side seam, using a 1cm seam allowance. Position the disc of fabric at the base of the tube with the right side facing in. Pin the edges of the circle and the base of the tube together. Cut little snips in the perimeter of the base of the tube of fabric every 3cm so that it splays out and the edges meet up. The fabric will probably need to be gathered a little so that the two pieces fit together – just spread it so that it doesn't suddenly bunch up at one point. Sew the sides together, using a 1cm seam allowance.

3 If you want, hem the top of the bag, or just leave it unfinished. Use a piece of ribbon or string, or a torn strip of fabric, to tie. Or make the fabric tie, below.

Alternatively, see the furoshiki bottle wrap on pages 132–33.

To make a fabric tie

Cut a piece of fabric just over twice the width that you want your tie to be. Fold it in half with the right sides facing in and machine stitch the raw edges together with a 0.5cm seam. Leave one of the short ends open. To turn the fabric the right way out, get some strong thread – embroidery thread is perfect – and anchor it firmly into the end of the tube that has been sewn shut, with a couple of stitches. Feed the needle along the inside of the tube and out the open end. Pull firmly on the needle, making sure it doesn't unthread, so that it brings the closed end of the fabric through the tube. You'll need to use your other hand to lightly hold the outside of the fabric, keeping it in place while the inside is dragged through. Help it on its way by pushing the outer fabric away from the needles as you pull. Neatly stitch the open end closed, with edges pushed in.

TIP

One of my favourite fabric tips is to tear material, rather than cut it, to get a perfectly straight edge. It only works on natural fabrics, though. Synthetic will not pull apart in the same way. Use scissors to cut a 2cm snip where you want to begin to tear the fabric and then just rip it in two. As well as creating a perfectly straight line, pulling the fibres apart in this way creates soft, frayed edges, which look fabulous on a tablecloth, napkin or anything else where you want to make a virtue of unfinished edges. Just pull away the long fibres to create a tufted fringe as wide as you want it. Tearing off thin strips of fabric is a brilliant quick and easy way to make your own ribbons. This works best on thinnish fabrics, as you can tear strips as narrow as you like.

SEW SIMPLE MAGNETIC SEWING KIT

Here's a nifty little way to stash the sewing bits and pieces that you need to hand when you're knitting or sewing, but that can easily get lost. This magnetic holder keeps everything together in one place – a darning needle for finishing off loose ends, little scissors to trim them, a few pins and safety pins, needles and thread, a little tape measure. So simple.

I have magnets dotted all over the place to hold pins and needles. There's a magnet with needle and thread attached next to the washing machine for emergency repairs to clothes when I'm laundering them. And I have magnets dotted on the metal lamp next to my sewing machine so that I'm not forever losing my needles.

you will need

Craft knife

Tape measure

A 30cm square of fabric, cut with pinking shears to stop fraying

1m ribbon

1 x A4 magnetic sheet

Double-sided tape

Method

1 First, use a craft knife to cut two parallel slits 2cm apart in the centre of the fabric square. They need to be wide enough to thread your ribbon through.

2 Thread the ribbon through the slits so that the long ends are on the right side of the fabric (if there is one) and pull it so that the middle is between the slits.

3 Now for the genius part – the magnet. Using scissors, cut a 10cm² piece from the magnetic sheet. Cover the back of the sheet with double-sided tape. Peel off the backing and centre the magnet on the wrong side of the fabric, over the narrow strip of ribbon – it will fix the ribbon in place to stop it pulling out.

4 Sprinkle pins and needles onto the magnet and whatever else you want to include in your sewing kit. Fold over the fabric to make a little parcel. Tie a bow with the ribbon to fix it. If the ends are too long, trim to size by folding the ribbon in half lengthways and cutting at a 45° angle with the blades pointing to the end of the ribbon, to give a professional-looking finish.

This is a gorgeous, brilliant, quick and easy present that any sewer or knitter would appreciate.

TIP If you don't have a cutting mat, keep polystyrene packaging from food, or anything else, to use as a base for cutting with a craft knife – the knife will sink into it without damaging surfaces.

COVERED NOTEBOOK

I love notebooks. I always have one by my side – in my handbag, next to my bed, in my car, on my desk. I can't imagine how anyone does without them. If I don't instantly make a note of something I want to remember, I WILL forget it. So everything – creative ideas, 'to do' lists, a date or place to remember, a recommendation – gets jotted down.

As I get through them fairly fast, I just buy cheapies for myself. I like to give them as gifts, though, in which case a cheapie won't really do, so it can end up being a simple present that doesn't look like much but actually costs rather a lot. And, as I discovered after I gave my mum a posh book, the recipient of an especially beautiful notebook might be reluctant to use it because it seems like a waste once it's finished. So, the thought of binding cheapies with leather offcuts or beautiful fabrics came about.

you will need

Cheap notebook – as small or as large as you want

Fabric or leather scraps – enough to cover the front, back and spine of the book (plus enough to cut a long thin strip to use as a tie)

Craft knife

Double-sided tape

Photographs (optional)

Method

1 It looks pretty to have a really long tie that winds around the book a couple of times before being tied in a bow, or if you prefer it can just go round once. If there's not enough leather, you could use a contrasting fabric or ribbon as the tie (you'll need to hem the ends of the ribbon, though, to stop it fraying). The beauty of using leather as the tie is that you just need to cut it – job done – it won't fray. If you are using fabric, see page 80 for how to make a fabric tie.

2 Place the fabric right side down on a cutting mat and position the book on top. Mark where the spine will go. Using a craft knife, make two small slits on the fabric next to each other just over halfway up where the spine will be. Weave the strip of fabric or leather through the slits, making sure it's centred.

3 Cover the entire outside cover of the notebook with double-sided tape. Remove the tape protector and lay it onto the fabric or leather, spine first. Trim the fabric or leather so it fits the book perfectly. Don't worry about the edges of the fabric fraying as the tape will hold it.

4 If you want to add a personal touch, print out photographs on normal (not photo) paper. Scale them so they will completely cover the page or the inside covers. The easiest way to stick them in is to push them up against the spine, then apply double-sided tape along the other three edges of the page or inside cover that the picture is to be stuck to. Remove the protective cover of the tape, a little at a time, pressing the picture flat over the tape as you go. Add in as many or as few photos as you like.

5 If you want, make a little slip cover of fabric. Cut two pieces large enough to cover the book, taking into account the depth of the book, and seam allowances, and sew three sides together.

6 Write or stamp a message on or inside the front cover.

For a super-cool personalised book cover, see the Gratitude journal under Thanksgiving on page 135. How to transfer a photograph onto fabric in seconds!

★ ★ ★
A PRETTY LINED PURSE

I am a sucker for little zipped-up purses – so pretty and so useful. I keep several in my bag – for coins, for receipts, to protect my camera and for make-up. It's so much easier to find something in a little purse rather than scattered loose in the cavernous depths of a bag. After a lot of playing around I finally stumbled upon this brilliant (though I say so myself) almost origami-like method of making a lined purse that looks fab.

you will need

Fabric cut into 4 rectangles measuring 16cm x 14cm. Use any fabric you like – mixed or matched

Sewing machine, thread and pins

Fabric scissors

12cm zip

1cm wide ribbon (optional)

✸ ✸ ✸ ✸ ✸ ✸ ✸
Zipper tassel

Loop thread 20 or 30 times through the hole at the end of the zipper pull, creating a loop of thread 2–3cm long. Wind more thread around the top, just below the zipper hole that the thread has gone through, to create a ball of thread at the top. Knot securely several times. Cut through the looped end of the thread and the tassel is created. Ta da!

✸ ✸ ✸ ✸ ✸ ✸ ✸

Method

1 Align two pieces of fabric with the right sides facing in. If you want the lining and outside of the purse to be made of contrasting fabrics, use two rectangles from each fabric. Make sure the matching pieces are together, so that when the pairs are placed on top of each other, you have two the same together. This way, when the right sides are flipped out, the lining will be all one fabric and the outer the other. Genius. The longer sides are the top and bottom of the purse. Fold out a 1cm hem along the top edges (see top left in picture, opposite). Pin or press to hold.

2 Repeat with the second two rectangles of fabric.

3 Next, put one pair on top of the other. Make sure the top edges are perfectly aligned.

4 Sew the four pieces together around three sides – leaving the top open – using a 1cm seam allowance. Once the edges are sewn, cut the point off the two bottom corners. This will give you sharp corners on the outside of the purse when you turn it the right way.

5 Now for the origami magic! Keep three pieces of fabric together and flip the fabrics so that the right sides are facing out, with three pieces together on one side and one on its own. Separate them so that you have two and two, and flip inside out again. Ta da! A lined purse, with a channel ready for the zip to slot in. If you want to switch the lining and outer fabric the other way round, just flip the purse inside out again to swap.

6 Slide the zip fabric into the lining, then pin it in positions and machine stitch it in. Leave a 1cm gap at each end of the zip. Get a little bit of 1cm wide ribbon, or a scrap of fabric (folded so that the raw ends are underneath, and position it over each end of the zip, tucking the edges into the channel where the zip has gone. Hand sew the rest of the lining and outer together, anchoring the ribbon or fabric firmly in. This will cover the ends of the zip and the gaps at each end for a really neat finish.

REVERSIBLE RIBBON-HANDLED BAG

These bags are made using the same origami-style flip trick as the zippered lined purses (see page 84), but actually they're even simpler, as you don't need to sew in a zip. They look fantastic and are so useful, they are one of my favourite things to make for friends. Plus, they are so easy to make...

you will need

4 rectangles of fabric (use 2 different fabrics and cut 2 from each) measuring approx. 40cm x 50cm. When I say approx., I really mean it. I make loads of these bags and they never come out the same size. It's not an exact science. So, cut your fabric to the size you like

Sewing machine, thread and pins

2.5m ribbon – whichever finish and width you like best

Fabric scissors

TIP

Don't forget – whenever you lift the foot on the sewing machine to turn the fabric, always make sure the machine needle is down and anchored firmly into the fabric, to hold it in place.

Method

1 As with the purse, sandwich the fabric together in two lots of two – matching fabrics together, with the right sides facing in (see steps 1–3 on page 84). Fold down 1cm at the top, folding outwards on each pair, and pin. This creates a channel for the ribbon handles to slip into.

2 Sew around three sides using a short stitch for strength. Leave the top with the folded hems open.

3 Flip the bag the right way round. You'll need to flip at least a couple of times – the first will leave three layers of fabric together, the second will leave two and two (see step 5 on page 84). If you would prefer the fabric that's ended up outside to be inside, just flip again.

4 Now for the ribbon straps. Cut the length of ribbon in two. The raw ends of each will go into the lining on each side of the bag – each end of the same length into the same side of the bag. Pin and sew around the top, anchoring the straps in place as you go. As before, use a short stitch for strength. After you have sewn all the way around the top of the bag, oversew the points where the ribbon is anchored into the lining to create a really strong bond. A rectangle with a cross is the traditional way of doing this. It looks professional, but all you need to know is how to do a forward and reverse stitch on your machine. Sew simple.

This bag is completely reversible. Just flip to have the fabric facing whichever way you like.

Totally. Love. It.

A SIMPLE CHARM BRACELET

This method offers a really easy way of making a bracelet, to which you can attach whatever you like – an engraved disc, a charm, a religious symbol – that is easy to take off, without having to add a clasp. Everyday, simple style.

you will need

Trinket or charm – whatever you want to attach

35cm of 1mm waxed cotton or thin leather cord. This is very cheap and, as usual, I find it easiest to buy online, although haberdashers and craft suppliers will stock it.

TIP

Charms make great gifts for every occasion – a four leaf clover for luck, a mini landmark charm to remember a special trip, a charm with a stork for a pregnancy gift, a vintage typewriter charm for a new job and so on. Online marketplaces have loads of old silver charms that cost very little to buy. If you want engraved or stamped discs, Etsy is a great place to find people who make them. Maybe get one with an initial, a quote or a date stamped on. Single or stacked, charms look fabulous on this simple yet elegant bracelet.

Method

1 Attach the charm to the cotton with a loose knot. Don't pull it tight at this stage because you might want to move the charm when the bracelet is finished to make sure it is centred. Make a large circle from the cotton, so that the loose end to your left, that loops towards the right, comes over the top of the circle.

2 Pinch the crossover point between your left forefinger and thumb and loop the right-hand loose end around the cotton three times, so that you have three smaller loops twisting around the circle.

3 Push the same loose end through the three little loops from left to right and pull so that it forms a knot with a triple loop.

4 Turn the bracelet over so that the unknotted loose end is on the right and repeat steps two and three. You will now find that pulling on the loose ends will tighten the bracelet, and stretching out the circle will enlarge it. At this stage, don't worry about the size. You will probably have very long loose ends, because it is easiest to tie the knots that way.

5 To make the bracelet the size you want, loosen off the triple knots and tighten again to leave a shorter piece of excess cotton. You might need to do this a few times until the circle is exactly as you want it, that is, easy to get over the hand, but without so much excess that it looks messy when the ends are pulled tight.

6 When the bracelet is the right size, finish off the ends by tying a single knot on each loose end 2mm away from the double knot. (No need to do this if you've used leather cord, because it won't fray). Cut off the excess length.

If you need to adjust the position of the charm, just loosen off the slip knot and re-tighten.

Make a pretty little fabric pouch (see page 79 for gift bags) to put the bracelet in.

✦✦✦ LEATHER CARD CASE

I have never found a wallet that has enough space for cash and cards, without being so enormous as to be almost a bag in itself. My solution is to keep coins and cards in small separate wallets, which I reckon is miles more practical and actually takes up less space in a handbag.

These little leather wallets are gorgeous and only take minutes to make. I'm not kidding – ten minutes max! They're not practical for coins, but perfect for cards.

you will need

Template (see page 155) and paper scissors

20cm x 22cm piece of leather for the wallet, plus enough to make a strap measuring at least 45cm x 0.5cm – longer if you want it to wrap around a couple of times. You can buy offcuts from leather suppliers or markets, but old clothes from jumble sales and thrift shops are also a good source of cheap leather.

Fabric scissors

Craft knife

PVA or other glue that will stick leather with a strong bond

Method

1 Cut out, or copy and cut out, the case template on page 155. Lay it on top of your piece of leather and cut around. The easiest way to hold the template in place is to clip the paper and the leather together with a few paperclips.

2 Mark two lines on the leather, as shown on the template, and then cut across them with a craft knife to make two small slits. This is to thread the leather strap through.

3 Fold up the bottom flap of the wallet and then fold in the two side flaps to make an envelope. Paint glue onto the underside of the side flaps where they will overlap the bottom flap and fix them into place. Press the pieces firmly together using your thumb and forefinger. Make sure the glue goes right to the ends of the raw edges. If glue oozes out along the edges, use something like a needle or a knife to scrape away the excess carefully so it won't leave any marks.

4 Cut a long, thin strip of leather to use as a tie measuring 45cm x 0.5cm or 65cm x 0.5cm, depending on whether you want the strap to wind around the wallet once or twice. Don't worry about a template or being too exact. Just go by eye, but cut carefully to keep the lines as straight as possible.

5 Once the glue has dried, thread the tie through the slits on the back of the purse. Fold over the top flap and wind the leather strap around and tie a bow. I like mixing up the colours, or going for metallic leathers, which look really smart.

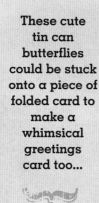

These cute
tin can
butterflies
could be stuck
onto a piece of
folded card to
make a
whimsical
greetings
card too...

PEPPERMINT AND LIME LIP BALM

Homemade lip balm makes a perfect little extra gift for a friend, or is ideal as a little thank you present. It's incredibly simple to make, and once you know how, you will never want to buy an overpriced pot of balm again.

This lip balm smells and tastes delicious. Unlike a lot of the stuff that we buy to put on our lips, it literally is good enough to eat, as it's made from only natural ingredients. It's also great for moisturising cuticles, dry skin on hands, and even your face – a real multi-tasker when you're out and about.

you will need

(for 1 small pot of lip balm)

1 heaped teaspoon refined shea butter

1 heaped teaspoon solid coconut oil

4 drops peppermint essential oil

8 drops lime essential oil

Suitable containers (see right)

Wire wool, paint (and small paintbrushes) or spray paint

Method

1 Put the shea butter and coconut oil in a clean heatproof bowl set over a pan of boiling water and heat to melt. Once they are about 50 per cent melted, take the bowl off the heat and stir well to melt all the solids. Now add the essential oils and mix.

2 Pour into a small, clean pot. Mini jam jars are perfect – the sort you get in hotels and restaurants. (In fact, those little jars are always useful. They are great for decanting small amounts of product for travelling so stash them whenever you can.)

3 If you're using a recycled jar, either sand or scrub the paint off the lid, or spray paint it. I scrubbed this lid using wire wool and then decorated it with little butterflies cut out from an old drinks tin using a butterfly punch, stuck on with superglue. If you're decorating the lid in this way, it's a good idea to make a little slip pouch to keep the pot in, to protect the butterflies.

NOTE: This lip balm will stay hard in the pot in temperatures up to about 23°C. In hotter weather than that, you might want to keep it in the fridge overnight.

TIP The thin metal used for soft drink cans is great for decorative use as it can easily be stamped or cut into shapes. Just cut the top and bottom off the can using sharp scissors, then cut down the side of the metal tube.

ROSE AND MANDARIN BATH OIL

This is a lovely oil to use every day. Just pour it straight into the bath, massage it onto your body before bathing to let it absorb, or rub it all over after a shower. The rose and mandarin combine beautifully to make a pretty, delicate scent.

you will need

200ml almond oil

10ml rose essential oil

10ml mandarin essential oil

(Alternative: grapefruit and neroli essential oils)

Pump dispenser or bottle

Fabric (optional) – for covering the dispenser

Polystyrene (optional) – for making a stamp

Fabric paint or eggshell (optional)

TIP

This oil works brilliantly as a face cleanser, too. Rub some all over your face and wash off with a damp muslin cloth. It will take off even the heaviest make-up, including waterproof mascara.

Method

1 Combine the almond and essential oils and decant into a pump dispenser or bottle. (See page 47 for advice on obtaining pump dispensers.)

2 If you are recycling a dispenser or bottle and want to cover it in fabric, why not go for a plain material and handprint it with an Indian printing block or a Paisley pattern? You can very easily make a rudimentary stamp using a piece of polystyrene – the round bases that come with shop-bought pizzas are perfect for this. Simply draw the outline of a Paisley shape onto the polystyrene. Use the tip of a pencil to press a dotted pattern inside the teardrop shape. Cut out around the outline. Then stamp away using fabric paint. You can actually use eggshell paint as an alternative for printing on fabric. I used it on my block printed pump dispenser on page 46. Just treat it as you would fabric paint. Leave to dry and fix it by covering with a cloth and going over with a very hot iron (no steam).

3 See page 47 for how to cover the pump dispenser with the fabric.

This is a beautiful looking and smelling bottle of perfumed oil to use whenever you feel in need of a little pampering or time out.

TIP
It fixes nail varnish, too! After painting nails (finished with a top coat of quick-dry varnish), leave them for a couple of minutes, then squirt some oil over the nails. After a couple more minutes they should be set hard.

Coconut and sugar body scrub

Mix equal amounts of desiccated coconut and caster sugar or brown sugar for an instant body scrub.
It's quick and easy to mix up and it leaves your body feeling invigorated, fresh and smooth. Use in the bath or shower. Heaven.

HOW TO MELT CHOCOLATE

Knowing how to melt chocolate properly, so that it hardens back into its original state, is a really useful trick to have up your sleeve, as it means you can melt down chocolate bars and re-form them into all sorts of brilliant gifts.

Method

The important thing is to melt the chocolate using as little heat as possible. This way, the temperature of the chocolate never gets above mildly lukewarm, which means it won't lose its 'temper'. Basically, this means that when it goes hard again, it will be just as shiny and snappy as it was before you started playing around with it. If you've melted chocolate before and it's not reset properly, looking dull and not properly hard, it's because it has become too warm during the melting process and consequently lost its temper.

The easiest way to melt chocolate is in a microwave. First, break your chocolate into small squares and keep a few back. Grate the extras into splintery shards using a knife. Zap the squares in 30-second bursts. Stir vigorously with a spatula between blasts, making sure as much chocolate as possible melts each time. It will make your arm ache a bit, but it's worth persisting to do it properly. Resist the temptation to let the microwave do the work. Once it's all melted, add the grated chocolate you kept back and stir it in to melt. This little trick makes doubly sure your chocolate will reset as it should (see the technical point below). If you don't have a microwave, heat the chocolate very gently in a bain-marie. The same principle applies about not raising the temperature of the chocolate too much. Take it off the heat and stir vigorously as soon as it starts to melt. Return it to the heat only intermittently if needed. Again, add the reserved shards of chocolate at the end, without returning to the heat. Remember – the key is melting the chocolate without ever letting it get too warm.

What is the temper?

The temper is basically the structure of chocolate. Chocolate is made up of crystals, constructed in a way that makes chocolate shiny and smooth and gives it its 'snap' when you break it. If the temper is lost (ie. the structure of the building blocks is changed) then its properties change and the chocolate looks dull and bends rather than breaks. Melting chocolate the correct way is a very technical business, involving heating it to a certain temperature and cooling it again to a specific temperature. The process corrals the crystals back into their correct alignment. The simple method given above prevents the temperature raising beyond a certain point and adding unmelted blocks at the end 'reminds' the melted chocolate of its correct form, so that, like sheep, any crystals that have got out of line should fall right back in.

CHOCOLATE PEANUTS, PUMPKIN SEEDS & RAISINS

These tempting treats are delicious, more-ish, make a great gift and are so simple they take seconds to prepare. They're a brilliant quick trick to have up your sleeve for when you suddenly realise you need a little gift to give to someone, because you can whip them up so speedily with a few store-cupboard basics. I love the combination of peanuts, pumpkin seeds and raisins, but you could use any mixture of nuts, seeds and dried fruit you have lurking in your cupboard.

 **you will need**

150g bar of good chocolate (milk, dark, white, whichever you prefer), broken into small pieces

150g natural roasted peanuts

75g pumpkin seeds

75g raisins

Suitable jars

Label maker (optional)

Luggage ties or labels and ribbon – for attaching to the jar

Method

1 Melt the chocolate (see opposite). Pour in the nuts and raisins and stir with a silicone spatula until all the dry ingredients are coated.

2 Pour out the mix onto a piece of non-stick baking paper and spread it out as thinly as you can. Leave to set.

4 Get a clean, dry jar. If you're reusing an old jar, you could prettify the lid with fabric. Cover the lid with double-sided tape and cut away the excess tape. Fix a piece of fabric over it and trim so that it overhangs as much as you like. If you have an embossed label maker, print out a label – either a greeting or the contents of the jar – and stick it onto the glass. If you don't have a label maker, a luggage label tied around the neck of the jar with a piece of ribbon or string looks great, too.

5 When the chocolate has set, break up the nuts by lifting the paper and cracking the layer of nuts from underneath, so the warmth of your hands doesn't melt the chocolate. Decant into the jar. Naturally, the quantity here is far too much for one jar, unless it's absolutely massive. You do want some leftovers for yourself, don't you?!

{ **TIP** Always use a silicone spatula when mixing. They scrape the bowl so effectively, no mix is wasted and it makes the washing up easier – win win! }

IRRESISTIBLE CHOCOLATE HONEYCOMB

Honeycomb is of those things that is surprisingly easy to make – its yumminess belies its simplicity. My favourite sort of gorgeous. That said, I did go through several days, and lots of frustrating failures, to finally come up with this version, so I would advise following the recipe closely.

I am such a mad fan of the powers of bicarbonate of soda, I couldn't write a book without including the wonderstuff in some way. And frankly, what could be a more seductive option than using it to create one of the most delicious sweet treats ever invented? Honeycomb... crunchy... hokey pokey... sponge candy... cinder toffee... fairy food candy... whatever you call it, I defy anyone to resist its charms.

✦ you will need

200g caster sugar

60g unsalted butter

60ml agave syrup – light or dark

2 teaspoons bicarbonate of soda (measure this out and put to one side before you start cooking, so it is there the second you need it)

250g chocolate

Method

OK, a couple of things. I know the agave syrup (sometimes called agave nectar) sounds a bit fancy, but having used the usual alternatives of honey and golden syrup, I think this is the best option by miles. It gives sweetness without being cloying. A light sweetness. You should be able to get it in most supermarkets or online. If you have difficulty getting hold of it, maple syrup is the best alternative. And butter? I know, it's not usual in honeycomb recipes, but it adds a clean melt-in-the-mouth quality, which means it doesn't stick to your teeth, as some versions do.

1 Line a roasting tin with non-stick baking paper and set aside. Put the sugar, butter and agave syrup in a large frying pan over a high heat. The reason for using a frying pan is so that the ingredients are spread as thinly as possible, so they melt evenly over the heat without the base of the honeycomb burning.

2 Leave without stirring for three minutes. If you can see areas burning around the edges, shake the pan or stir very gently. After three minutes, use a silicone spatula to mix it all together well to disperse the heat.

3 Leave for another minute or so, or until all the sugar is melted and the mixture is translucent and lightly golden and there are small bubbles throughout the mix – whichever comes sooner. Don't let it burn. This is important because adding the bicarb makes the sugar brown even more, so there's a very fine line between golden perfection and overdone. As soon as the optimum melting point is reached, take the pan off the heat. Sprinkle the bicarb over and whisk it in super fast with a balloon whisk.

4 Pour the frothy mix into the lined tin and leave to set. It should continue to rise as it cools. Leave to cool completely, then break into chunks.

5 Now melt your chocolate (see the 'how to' on page 96). Dip the pieces of honeycomb into the melted chocolate and place on a piece of non-stick baking paper to set. When the chocolate is completely set, transfer to a jar for giving. Don't worry; this recipe makes loads, so there will be plenty of leftovers for you... Heaven on a plate!

Smash some of this up and add it to vanilla ice cream for a delicious pudding!

'BREAKFAST IN BED' TRAY

Old wooden potato trays make great oversized 'breakfast in bed' trays. The present-giving opportunities of something so appealing are pretty limitless – Valentines, a birthday, a wedding, a wedding anniversary, Mother's Day, Father's Day... I mean, who doesn't like breakfast in bed?

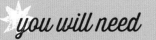

you will need

An old potato tray – see resources, page 157

Sandpaper, medium grade

Paint – preferably eggshell

Roller and small paintbrush

Luggage label and pen or paints and paintbrush

Ribbon or string

Present inspiration

If you're giving it as a present to others, why not parcel up the tray with some (or all, depending on how generous you're feeling) of the following... a couple of vintage plates, tea cups, a little vase, a tea pot, a jug. Hunt down pretty bargains that are cheap and cheerful. Any time you're at a boot fair or a market, a second-hand store or browsing online, just keep an eye out for bits you like and build up a little stash.

Method

1 As potato crates have been used for storing potatoes, yours might be pretty dirty and may have been stored somewhere damp, so the first thing to do is to leave the tray standing on its side for a couple of days, just to be sure it's dried out. Then give it a really good sand, to clean off all the dirt and make the tray smooth. An electric sander will do the job super-fast if you have one. If not, doing it by hand isn't too arduous. Always wrap sandpaper around a cork block for hand sanding. It makes the job so much easier. Vacuum away all the dust to get it ready for painting.

2 As usual, I think it's easiest to paint with a roller, for speed and finish. You will need a brush, too, though, for the fiddly bits the roller won't reach. Raise the tray off the surface you're working on with little blocks or bricks so that it doesn't stick to it. Leave to dry completely.

3 Print or write the breakfast in bed quote (see opposite) or any other quote or message you like onto a luggage label and attach it to the tray with ribbon or string.

If you're serving up the breakfast yourself, remember...

Don't fill cups and mugs as high as normal when serving breakfast in bed, and forget about long-stemmed glasses. You don't want to create another job of having to change the bedding afterwards thanks to spills all over it. As the base is slatted, lay a pretty tea towel or piece of fabric on the inside of the tray to catch crumbs.

(Please note: the beauty of this tray is its size. Unfortunately, staircases and doorways aren't designed for its majestic proportions – unless you happen to live somewhere very grand – so rotate it 90° before carrying).

When not deployed on romantic ventures, these oversized trays look gorgeous on top of an upholstered coffee table (like the 'fur coat, no knickers' pallet table on page 25) or just propped against the kitchen wall ready to use for TV dinners, or a picnic lunch in the garden.

'Breakfast in bed,
and a kiss or three...'
Eddie Hinton and Donnie Fritts

'WEAR YOUR HEART ON YOUR SLEEVE' ENGAGEMENT RING GLOVES

These gloves make a sweet, whimsical present for a newly engaged girlfriend. Of course, an engagement is not an occasion that absolutely requires you to give a gift, but when a friend of mine got engaged in wintertime, it got me thinking. When you've got news to tell, you want to show it off, don't you...

you will need

A pair of gloves – any old pair will do

Sewing needle and gold or silver thread

A sew-on crystal – you can easily buy these, but old clothes and cheap jewellery are a good source, too. I culled a load of cheap rhinestones from an old sparkly top I no longer wore

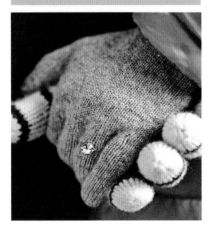

... I remember the lurch of excitement every time I'd glance down and catch sight of the sparkler sitting on my ring finger when it was all shiny and new. So, I thought a pair of gloves that don't cover up your big news would be quite fun.

They're very easy to make, because I'm not suggesting you actually knit the gloves yourself (in which case, they might just be ready in time for the first wedding anniversary).

Method

First of all, sew a running stitch around the ring finger of the glove, to mark the position of the ring. Then go over it with 1mm width over-stitches, tight together. Once the shiny band is finished, position the sparkler and sew it in place. Put on the gloves – just to check, of course – admire, enjoy... then hand them over!

You could offer to update the gloves after the wedding by detaching the stone and turning the band into a wedding ring.

PERSONALISED PICNIC BLANKET

Along with chocolate, blankets are one of those things I can never resist. The thing that connects them both is comfort. I have so many blankets – folded and slung over the backs and arms of sofas, on chairs around the kitchen table, along the bottom of beds – always on hand for cosy warmth. This lovely picnic blanket makes a great gift that can be used indoors and out. Perfect for eating al fresco on hot summer days or snuggling under on cold winter nights.

you will need

Blanket – personally, I prefer old, second-hand and vintage (which is just another word for second-hand, of course, but it sounds so much posher). Main reason? Because you can pick up real bargains, of course. My best tip – the greatest source of fabulous old blankets... ex-military. These are made to be thick and tough enough to keep soldiers warm in the most inhospitable of environments. Churned out in bulk, they offer a cheap and plentiful supply of thick wool, almost felted, oversized blankets. Absolutely fabulous.

Fabric – for personalising the blanket

Letter templates (see right)

Pins

Fabric scissors

Sewing needle and thread

Method

1 One downside of buying old blankets is that they may have been stored in mothballs for protection. If so, you'll need to get rid of that smell first. The most effective way is to wash on a wool cycle, putting a cupful of soda crystals and a couple of teaspoons of bicarbonate of soda in the detergent drawer, and white vinegar (see resources, page 157) in the softener compartment. Bicarb is brilliant at getting rid of bad smells and vinegar is a fantastic natural softener. Dry outside in the fresh air. You might need to repeat if the smell is really ingrained.

2 To personalise the blanket, cut out letters in a pretty fabric, to spell out a word or family name – or Mr and Mrs if it's for newly-weds. The easiest way to make your letter templates is to find a lettering design you like online, scale it up to the size you want, print it out and cut it out. Pin it onto the fabric and then cut around. The only downside of sewing onto a thick woollen blanket is it's tricky to do on a sewing machine as the fabric is so bulky, so this is a job that does really need to be done by hand. Hopefully the recipient doesn't have too long a name...

3 Don't worry about the raw edges of the fabric. No need to turn them under. Just use blanket stitch, which will protect the edges from fraying too much. Plus it has a pleasing homespun quality.

4 To package up your customised blanket, tear a strip of the same fabric you've used for the letters. Tie around your folded blanket, like an old parcel.

The comforting softness of a picnic blanket on prickly, dry grass on a scorching hot day makes this a present that will be enjoyed for years to come.

BIKE-SEAT COVER

A bicycle seat cover is a very practical and useful present for anyone you know who cycles. Who wouldn't be delighted to swap this for the hotel shower cap option most cyclists go for. There's nothing wrong with those. They're practical, serviceable and free. But in the style stakes, you can't beat one of these, and happily they don't require an awful lot more effort than snaffling the hotel freebies next time you're on holiday, which, clearly, you wouldn't give as a present anyway. Would you?

you will need

A piece of oilcloth that's large enough to cover the template

Template (see page 156)

Fabric marker

Fabric scissors

Pins

Sewing machine and thread

½ m of 1cm-width elastic

TIP

You can use a safety pin to feed your elastic through the stitched channel. But for very little cost, you can buy a bodkin, which will zip through even the narrowest channel.

Method

1 Place the oilcloth on a work surface with the right side facing down. Place the template on the oilcloth and trace around the shape with the fabric marker. Cut out the shape. Fold in a 2cm hem and pin all the way around. Where the fabric bunches at a corner, cut snips into it.

2 Sewing oilcloth on a machine, with the right sides facing out, can be tricky as the rubbery fabric doesn't slide very well. Fix this by rubbing a teensy amount of baby oil on both sides of the hem before sewing it. That way, the fabric will glide under the needle smoothly, no problem. Whizz around the hem on the sewing machine. Leave a 2cm gap between the start and end points to allow you to thread the elastic through the hem later.

3 Now thread the elastic through the channel created in the hem (see tip, left). If you don't have a bodkin you could use a safety pin. Just pin it to the end of the elastic and feed the safety pin through the channel, pulling the elastic through with it. Once the elastic is threaded through, tie a loose looped knot that can easily be undone with the two ends of elastic. This is because bike seats do vary in shape and size, so the lucky recipient of your largesse can pull it to fit and then knot securely in place. The elastic should be pulled taut enough to hold, but not so tight that the cover shrink-fits onto the seat and won't be easily taken off when it's done its duty of protecting the saddle from inclement weather. Bring on the rain.

TIP A couple of pegs make brilliant bike clips for your trousers. How about covering each side of a peg with fabric to match the seat cover – just fix on with double-sided tape.

For me, turning a regular meal into a celebration can be as simple as tearing a rectangle of fabric to cover the kitchen table and adding a few lit candles. The point is, a celebration is about the people you are with plus some little extra touches that need not cost much money or take much effort, but signal that the occasion is special. Celebrating should be a pleasure for everyone, not a source of stress for you, the host.

Aside from the pressure we can put ourselves under when planning celebrations, there's also the cost. As with any money-making opportunity, some holidays have become so commercialised they end up putting us under a lot of pressure to overspend. Food, decorations, presents – it quickly adds up.

You think, 'Oh it's only once a year...' as you spend again – and again. It's only after the twinkliness disappears into a stretch of 300-odd days until it hits again (and the purchases that seemed so worth the money at the time have long been forgotten) that you remember what you thought you'd learned last year but promptly forgot. IT'S NOT ABOUT THE MONEY! So, take off the holiday goggles. The beauty of simple style is that it doesn't cost much.

This section of the book is made up of a mix of some traditional celebration foods, celebratory traditions and decorating touches. Two themes bind most celebrations: giving thanks and new life (or looking to the future). Whether you are secular or religious, whatever culture or background you are from, they are sentiments that sustain us all.

I am fascinated by how others celebrate. I love coming across something in another culture that I didn't know about before, and it's so fantastic I just want to embrace it and pass it on.

Each item in this section is pegged to the different celebration that inspired it. But everything can be used or done, at any time of year, by anyone. These are, quite simply, special things I make and do, and love... for sharing, for giving, for celebrating...

EASTER

Easter Sunday falls on the first Sunday after the full moon that falls on or after 21st March – hence, it falls in either March or April. A period of Lent marks the countdown to Easter and includes the days that mark the anniversary of the crucifixion of Christ. Easter Sunday commemorates the resurrection of Jesus, although, as with Christmas, many people celebrate without giving much thought to the religious meaning of the celebration.

GOLDEN CHOCOLATE EGGS

Chocolate eggs are a traditional Easter gift in many countries – but why eggs? They are a symbol of new life and, for Christians, a reminder of the resurrection of Jesus. However, Easter was originally a Pagan festival to celebrate Eostra, the goddess of spring and fertility – hence the Easter bunny and chicks being part of the celebrations today.

you will need

Chocolate – white, plain or dark. About 70g for a small egg (the size of a duck egg), 150g for medium-sized and 250g for large

Plastic egg moulds

Edible gold dust – for the finish

Small treats to put inside (optional)

Small paintbrush

Clear cellophane – to wrap the eggs

Ribbon or gold thread

Making chocolate eggs at home is one of those things that sounds rather laborious and like far more effort than it is worth. Actually, if you know how to temper chocolate (see page 96), it is simple to do and the reward is so much greater than the time you put in. Especially if you have a cheeky little trick that makes your own creations look amazing. These are beautiful!

Method

① Melt the chocolate according to the guidance on page 96. It is vital the chocolate doesn't lose its temper or you'll be wasting your efforts and cash, because it just won't reset properly. Luckily it's almost as easy to melt it the right way as the wrong.

② Make sure your moulds are completely clean and dry before adding chocolate. Don't worry about oiling them as the chocolate will pop out easily when it hardens. A quick tap with a blunt knife will knock it out if it doesn't drop out. If you've ever put melted chocolate in a mould before and it hasn't come out easily, it's because the temper had gone. ☞

3 Before you put any chocolate into the moulds, coat them in edible gold dust. Put about ¼ teaspoon of dust into each shell and tip it around so that it lines the mould. Tip out any excess. It doesn't have to be uniform – as with everything homemade, disuniformity is good.

4 Pour about two tablespoons (don't measure, just pour and go by eye) of melted chocolate into each half of the shell and use a teaspoon to spread it around so that the mould is covered. Pop them in the fridge for 40 seconds or so, so the chocolate hardens. Keep stirring the melted chocolate meanwhile, to stop it stiffening.

5 Repeat the process until all the chocolate has been used except for a little that should be kept back to glue the shell halves together. Refrigerate.

6 Once the halves are set and before you stick them together, you can put little treats inside if you want to.

7 The easiest way to glue the chocolate shell halves together is to paint a thick coat of melted chocolate over the rim of one half. Sandwich both together and then use your finger to rub extra chocolate over any gaps. Don't worry if it looks slightly messy as the finishing touch will hide it.

8 Dip a clean, dry paintbrush in the gold dust and paint it over the chocolate join, so that it blends into the golden shells. You can paint a little extra gold dust over the outer shell for extra glitz.

9 Use clear cellophane to wrap the egg and tie around the top with some pretty ribbon or golden thread.

> **How fabulous does that look? For little more than the cost of a chocolate bar, a splendid golden egg that looks like it's come straight out of a top chocolatier. Love it!**

SPECKLED GANACHE EGGS

These eggs look super posh, taste delicious and make lovely gifts. And you can use the recipe for any celebration – just use mould shapes that suit the occasion. These eggs look gorgeous packed in quails' egg boxes, if you can get hold of them. Otherwise use cellophane bags tied with pretty ribbons.

you will need

For 20 half shells – 10 eggs

FOR THE GANACHE

75g white chocolate

75g dark chocolate (70% cocoa solids)

150ml double cream

Generous pinch of salt

FOR THE CHOCOLATE CASE

30g milk chocolate

150g white chocolate

Mini plastic egg moulds

Suitable containers (quails' egg boxes are good) or cellophane

Ribbon – to tie

TIP

Any leftover ganache can be kept in a jar and refrigerated. It's delicious spread on toast for a super-luxurious treat. You can also roll it into balls and roll in a mix of cocoa powder and edible gold glitter for some rather splendid dinner party truffles.

Method

1 For the ganache, first break up the white and dark chocolate. Add them to the cream and salt in a saucepan and heat over a fairly low heat. Stir constantly with a balloon whisk until the chocolate has completely melted. Take off the heat and continue to whisk furiously until the ganache is about twice as thick as it was when it came off the heat. Put to one side to cool.

2 For the case, break up the milk chocolate. Follow the 'how to temper chocolate' instructions on page 96 to melt it. Don't worry, tempering chocolate is not difficult, but it is super important! For this small amount, microwave in short 20-second bursts.

3 With a fine brush, paint little dots of melted chocolate into the egg moulds. You can also use a thicker brush to stipple chocolate into the moulds for a more dappled effect. Cheap children's paintbrushes are perfect for this. Refrigerate the painted mould while you melt the white chocolate, again using the tempering method on page 96.

4 Use a thick brush to paint a layer of white chocolate over the brown dots or specks. Refrigerate the mould to harden the chocolate for 30 seconds. Remove and paint another, thicker layer on. Scoop a generous amount of chocolate onto the brush so that it builds up a thick shell. Cover the remaining white chocolate and keep – you'll need it later to glue the egg halves together. Refrigerate the moulds until the chocolate is hard.

5 Once the shells are hard, fill with ganache to just below the rim of the mould. Refrigerate until the ganache has set firm. Leave it for at least a couple of hours. I tend to make these before bed, so they can be left overnight.

6 Tip the shell halves out of the moulds. They will fall out or come out easily with a sharp knock.

7 Very gently re-melt the white chocolate by heating it in 20-second bursts in the microwave and stirring vigorously to disperse the heat. Paint a layer on the top of the two egg halves, then press them together to fix. Repeat until all the shells are joined. Refrigerate to allow the joins to set hard.

NO-STRESS PANCAKES

Mardi Gras, Fat Tuesday, Shrove Tuesday, Pancake Day – the day before Lent traditionally begins with the rich ingredients in the home being used up to clear out the cupboards in readiness for a period of abstinence. Depending on where you are, the tradition means different ingredients to be used up and different recipes. In our house, as in so many others, it means one thing – pancakes!

I call these 'no-stress' pancakes because these are perfect every time, and are so simple to whip up any time for a quick, easy meal. I used to find making pancakes inexplicably tortuous. The first pancake would always stick, they would be too fat, too rubbery, never quite right.

The quantity here will make 8–10 large pancakes, more if they are smaller ones. Of course, the pancake size does depend on the size of your pan.

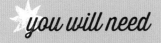

you will need

250g plain flour

350ml milk

3 eggs

Generous pinch of salt

2 dessertspoons caster sugar (optional) – leave out for savoury pancakes

90g unsalted butter

50ml water

2 tablespoons sunflower oil (or other light oil) in a small bowl and a clean cloth

Method

❶ Put the flour, milk, eggs, salt and sugar (if using) into a mixer bowl. Combine with a fork before whisking. After a minute of whisking, stop for a moment to scrape the sides and bottom of the bowl with a spatula, then carry on whisking. You want a completely smooth batter with no lumps. If you're using a freestanding mixer, leave it mixing from this point right up until you're ready to makes the pancakes – about eight minutes or so.

❷ Put the butter on to melt, and keep whisking the batter while the butter heats. Keep an eye on the butter to make sure it doesn't burn.

❸ When the butter has melted, ltake it off the heat and leave for a minute or so to cool slightly. Keep on whisking the batter all the time. One of the secrets of these delicious pancakes is the constant whisking – it keeps the mix light and makes the pancakes soft and fluffy. Still whisking the batter, add the butter very slowly – almost drop by drop – to incorporate it well into the mix. Don't add the milk solids left in the bottom of the pan. Whisk for a further couple of minutes. Add the water and whisk in.

❹ Pour the batter into a jug. I use a measuring jug to give me an idea initially of how much batter to pour out for each pancake (about 75ml) but then just go by eye. You need less mix than you think as it spreads so thinly.

❺ Put the frying pan over a high heat and let it get hot before you add any oil. Wipe a tiny amount of oil around the inside of the pan, applying just enough oil to coat it very lightly. When the pan is hot, pour in a portion of the mix. Use one hand to pour and the other to tilt the pan as the mix goes in, to swirl it around and get a thin coat over the entire pan. I lift the pan right up and onto its side as I tilt and turn, to make sure the mix spreads evenly.

❻ Put it back on the heat. Within about 20 seconds, the edges of the pancake will start to brown and peel away from the pan. Turn – or flip! – it at this stage. Cook the other side for about 40 seconds. Again, go by eye. The second side won't brown as much as the first, but you can see when the batter is cooked through. Once the pancake is cooked, repeat until all the batter is used up. Pile the pancakes onto a plate as you go. Keep them covered with a tea-towel to keep them warm, then serve.

NOTE

As with so many of the best seasonal offerings, they're great all year round – and they can be eaten sweet or savoury for breakfast, lunch or supper. Thinking about it, is there a more versatile recipe?!

TIP

ALTERNATIVE: You can use eggshells any time as a cute vase for little cut flowers by just adding water. They're perfect for when the children hand over a stubby bunch of wildflowers, plucked too short to stand in a vase.

LILY OF THE VALLEY EGGS

Giving Lily of the Valley is a May Day tradition in France that dates back to the sixteenth century, when King Charles IX began giving it to the ladies of his court as a lucky charm on the first of May. Today, in the run up to *La Fête du Travail* (Labour Day), the beautifully scented flowers are everywhere and can be picked up on street corners and in supermarkets and florists. Here's an idea for creating a gift to show affection and appreciation.

you will need

Eggs – if you can get them, duck eggs are perfect for planters as they are larger than hens' eggs and the white shells look beautiful. Otherwise, use the largest hens' eggs you can find. If you want to scale up, you can even go for goose eggs, which are really big, but they are hard to get and expensive, so the other options are more practical

Soil and moss

Lily of the Valley – perfect for planting in eggshells because the bulb is so small it will easily fit. If you can't get them, or want to use something else, make sure the bulb is small enough, or it has shallow roots that will be happy with little room. Grape hyacinths and snowdrops are great options

Egg cups or small glass jars

In a slight deviation from the French tradition, I like to have the wild spring flowers at home over Easter as they look so pretty in eggshells with the tiny, delicate, fragrant flowers, perfectly in proportion with the little, equally delicate container.

If you can get cut Lily of the Valley, just put the stems in eggshells with water. If not, you can buy 'pips' (small bulbs) from a garden centre or online, which can be planted in the shells.

Method

❶ Break off the top quarter of the shell. Hold the egg firmly and whack the shell smartly with a sharp knife to crack a clean line. A swift blow is better than little taps, which will cause lots of hairline fractures. Pick the top off carefully, so you don't crack the rest of the shell. Pour the eggs into a bowl – you can scramble them or make an omelette later. Rinse out the shells.

❷ Put some soil into the bottom half of the shell. Add a plant and press in. Finish off with some moss around the stem, if you can get some.

❸ Sit the eggs in egg cups or small glass jars and cluster together, or dot around.

❹ Water daily, but don't overwater – just make sure the soil always feels damp.

TIP If you have a cat and use litter made from silica or mineral granules, you can use it as a soil alternative in pots for plants. It retains water and drains well.

EID-AL-FITR

Celebrated after the end of the ninth month in the Muslim calendar – the holy month of Ramadan. Each year Ramadan begins 11 days earlier than the previous one, which means it falls in each of the months of the Western (or Gregorian) calendar over a period of 33 years.

BAKLAVA

Baklava is deceptively simple to make, especially if you go for this corner-cutting version that whittles the making process down to minutes. Some baklava recipes are very time-consuming, so naturally I wanted to come up with a super simple, speedy option. This one is so easy you can produce it effortlessly any time – for a celebration, for giving or just for a treat.

you will need

500g unsalted butter

175g pecans

175g shelled pistachios

(or any other combination of nuts you have to hand)

500g filo pastry

225ml agave syrup – or make up 225ml syrup with 175ml light runny honey combined with 40ml boiling water and 10ml orange flower water or rosewater and leave to cool

Method

1 Preheat the oven to 200°C, gas mark 6.

2 Line a 28cm x 40cm baking tin with non-stick baking paper.

3 Melt the butter over a low heat, taking care not to let it discolour and burn. Once most of it has melted you can take it off the heat and the residual heat in the pan should be enough to finish it off. You actually want clarified butter, which I always think sounds very cheffy and a little bit scary. But don't worry – there's a quick way of making a version. Not perfect, but good enough. Lay a tea-towel or muslin over the top of a bowl. Pour the melted butter into it. The milk solids – or at least most of them – will be caught by the fabric, allowing the golden liquid to pass through. Simple.

4 Blitz your nuts in a blender until they're finely ground but not like dust. Turn off the blender when you can still see some small chopped pieces and you should have a nice mix of textures. Mix the nuts with a generous pinch of salt and about 100g of the melted butter.

5 Unroll the filo pastry so it lies flat. To cut the pastry to fit the tin, place the pan gently on top of the pastry and cut around it with a sharp knife. Before ditching the offcuts, scrunch them up like a cloth and use them to spread about two tablespoons of the clarified butter over the baking paper in the tin.

6 Take a third of the filo pastry and lay it in the bottom of the tin. Sprinkle half the nut mixture over the pastry and spread it out evenly. Place another third of the pastry on top and repeat with the remaining nut mixture. Finally, place the last third of the pastry on top.

7 Now, you will notice we've not done the rather laborious task of brushing every single layer of filo pastry with butter. Don't worry. Time-saving masterstroke coming up...

8 Use a small sharp knife to cut through the uncooked pastry, making rectangles of about 3cm x 4cm. To make sure you cut right to the edge of the pastry, turn the pan so that you can put the blade in at the edge of the dough and cut towards you. Press the knife down rather than pulling it, to avoid dragging on the pastry and tearing it.

9 Once the pastry's cut, drizzle the rest of the clarified butter over the dough, making sure it's spread evenly. The pastry and nuts will absorb the butter like blotting paper. This is just as effective as brushing each layer of pastry with butter, but MILES quicker and much less faff. Make sure all the pastry is saturated with butter, but that there is no excess. You might not need to use all the butter. If you see it pooling anywhere, pick the pan up and tip it gently to spread it around until it's fully absorbed.

10 Put the baking tin in the oven for 15 minutes. If the baklava is all pale golden brown after that time, it's done. If there are still white bits, leave it for longer, in which case, turn the temperature down to 150°C and check after another five minutes, when it should be ready.

11 When the pastry is all gloriously golden and crisped up, remove from the oven and instantly drizzle over the syrup. Go slowly, to make sure every bit of the pastry is covered. I use agave syrup for this because I like the fact that it has a neutral taste, so adds sweetness without a strong flavour. If you can't get it in your supermarket, you should be able to buy it online. If not, the honey and rosewater/orange water mix (see opposite) is a great substitute, and is actually closer to the syrup used in traditional baklava recipes.

12 Cover the tin with tea-towels and leave to cool. The sugar syrup will be absorbed by the buttery, nutty pastry, adding a gooey moistness to the crispness of the delicate filo. This baklava is good the day you make it. It is even better the day after, and the one after that, as the ingredients continue to meld and the crispy pastry continues to absorb the syrup and butter. Divine.

★ ★ ★

Nothing may be consumed between dawn and dusk during Ramadan, so it is not surprising that Eid-al-Fitr, which literally means the Festival of Breaking Fast, is a time to indulge. Unlike Lent for Christians, observing the Ramadan fast is not an optional extra, but an enforced period to slow down, reflect and be grateful. Self-imposed deprivation requires great willpower. So, after a month of restriction, it's only natural that the sense of achievement is celebrated with some indulgence. What could be a more delicious treat than divine sweet baklava, which is eaten all year round, but has a special place on many Eid tables.

★ ★ ★

DIWALI

The Festival of Lights involves five days of celebrations and usually falls during October or November – the date is set by the Hindu calendar. Each of the days celebrates a different legend and the stories vary in different areas, but at the heart of the festivities is the triumph of good over evil – light over dark – hope. Light is essential to the celebrations.

HANGING FIREFLY GLASS LANTERNS

During Diwali homes are festooned with candles to help guide Lakshmi, the goddess of wealth, in.

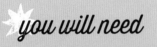

you will need

Muslin

Fabric scissors

Old glass jars

White fabric (optional)

Double-sided tape

Battery-operated tea lights – 1 for each lantern

Method

❶ Cut a square of muslin big enough to cover the lid and overhang the jar. Between 10cm and 15cm square should be good, depending on the size of the jar. Place the muslin over the top of the lid. If you can see the original colour of the lid through the muslin and it bothers you, cover the lid in double-sided tape and stick a piece of white fabric over it first. Anchor the muslin over the lid by fixing it with a piece of double-sided tape.

❷ Switch on a battery-operated tea light and put it inside the glass jar. Screw on the lid so that the cloth hangs down, covering the jar.

❸ To make the hanging loop, cut or tear a strip of muslin measuring approx 30cm x 2cm. Loop it around the neck of the jar and secure with a slip knot. Now take the long loose end over to the opposite side of the neck of the jar, so that a long loop is formed over the lid. Push the end under the fabric tied around the jar and secure with a looped slip knot. You can easily undo and redo the hanging loop when you want to take off the lid to turn the light on or off. So pretty!